IRIS
THE VINDICATOR

Herald Publishing House, Independence, Missouri

COPYRIGHT © 1977
Iris Griffiths Johnston

All rights in this book are reserved. No part of the text may be reproduced in any form without written permission of the publishers, except brief quotations used in connection with reviews in magazines or newspapers.

Library of Congress Cataloging in Publication Data

Griffiths, Iris.
  The Vindicator.

  SUMMARY: A biography of the Welsh immigrant to Utah whose disillusionment leads him to California where he finds the Reorganized Church and serves as its missionary to Wales.
  1. Griffiths, John, 1826-1891. 2. Mormons and Mormonism in the United States—Biography. 3. Missionaries—Wales—Biography. 4. Missionaries—United States—Biography. [1. Griffiths, John, 1826-1891. 2. Mormons and Mormonism in the United States—Biography. 3. Missionaries] I. Title.
BX8678.G74G74   289.3'3   [B]   [92]   77-1808
ISBN 0-8309-0172-8

Printed in the United States of America

THE VINDICATOR

THE VINDICATOR

This story centers around the life of a young man whose only wish was to live according to his own desires. Refusing to bow down to the Welsh nobility, he came to America. Freedom, he soon learned, was something he had to fight for wherever he was. He traveled west to Salt Lake Territory and was separated from the woman he loved. Warmed by the friendly reception of the Mormons, he worked willingly and gained great favor, soon climbing to a high position in the church. Slowly, however, as new doctrines were adopted, he began to see it as not as it had appeared at first. When he refused to carry out orders that would torment his conscience, he was threatened and held prisoner. He and his wife and children fled in the night. They crossed the desert in the heat of summer and through Indian country ill prepared for the great hardships they suffered. At last they reached California where they found a measure of security and a new faith.

The Vindicator deals with a family's confrontation with life and its many problems. It is a touching story of hope and frustration, achievement and defeat, love and loss—an account of pioneer America never before told.

John and Mary Griffiths

CHAPTER ONE

John Griffiths pumped water from the well and splashed some on his swollen, bloody face. He had just gotten into a brawl, and now that the heat of the moment had passed, he regretted his behavior. With one blow he had jeopardized his very life.

John had arisen early that morning, as usual. The sun was just beginning to rise, casting a golden glow across the meadows that are verdant in Wales throughout the year, watered by the mist blown inland from the sea. It was springtime, and in Wales after the long, cold, foggy winters spring was like an inspiration.

That morning John had walked along, kicking into the sod with the heel of his homemade brogan, then picking up a clod and crumbling it in his hand to see if the earth was ready to till. It was of the right firmness, so he had hitched his one horse to the plow.

After an hour John stopped at the end of a furrow and removed his tattered cap. An unruly strand of dark hair tumbled across his forehead, and he wiped it back with his sleeve. While letting the horse rest, he scanned the countryside and noticed a rider approaching in the distance. He could tell by the habit that he was of the nobility, probably one of the owners of the land John leased.

Landlords were hard on peasants. The rentals collected from John were more than half of what he made, and the tithes to the Church of England took a goodly share of what was left. He and his young wife had almost nothing to live on. Under English law it was nearly impossible for peasants to own land. They must lease it from the vast holdings of the aristocracy.

"How I hate those bloody lords!" John muttered, as the man drew nearer.

All commoners were expected to fall on their knees and bare their heads as a nobleman passed by. Defiantly, John did neither. As the rider approached, John recognized him as the young aristocrat who was next in line for the lordship and heir to all the land in this valley. He was near John's own age, overbearing, and often unkind to the peasants.

The nobleman rode by John, then turned his mount about and rode back slowly, closer to the field where John plowed. John continued to ignore him. He rode past twice, then a third time, before he drew rein and shouted: "Ho there, you peasant! Do you not see a nobleman and your superior passing?"

"I see a fine horse, sir, and the jockey who parades him past my field. What more is there for an honest man to see?" John replied. He drew up his horse and stood leaning on the fence facing the aristocrat, who was dressed in a red and gold riding habit.

"Down on your knees and off with your cap, you scum!" the nobleman shouted angrily.

John started to reply, thinking here was his opportunity to discuss some of the problems of the people with a future landowner, but he hardly got a word out.

"How dare you speak to me, you dirty plowhand!" The young nobleman rode closer to the fence and with all his might lashed John sharply across his face with his riding quirt.

John was so furious he lost all sense of reasoning or fear. He felt neither the sting of the whip nor the tiny drops of blood that trickled down from the cut across his face. With one great bound he was over the fence. He jerked the young man from his saddle and with one powerful blow sent him staggering to the ground.

The young man rolled in the dirt shouting, "You bastard, you'll hang for this!"

"What if I do? Is that any worse than being a slave? You are either going to listen to what I have to say or fight."

The arisotcrat made no attempt to rise.

"I cannot hit a coward who will not fight back," John said, and as he spoke he reached down and pulled the cowering man to his feet. Then he shoved him toward his horse that had been trained, as the peasants had, to stand at obedience.

"You can be thankful for the opportunity to depart unhurt. Mine may be the first hand to strike back in our defense, but it will not be the last. Your high and mighty father can take this land and keep it for all of me. There must be some place in the world where a common man can live in dignity and peace!" As John watched the disheveled young man ride away he was suddenly filled with fear. If only he had removed his cap and saluted the young lord—but he hadn't. And now his very life was in danger.

After John had washed the blood and dirt from his face he made his way cross-country to the neighbor he trusted most. Mr. Meddleson stood watering his team at the trough in the barnyard when he saw John approaching.

"Why all the haste, me lad?" He noticed John's appearance and added, "I pray ye do not bear bad news."

"Perhaps. That remains to be seen," John replied. "I just struck the young landlord that gives us so much trouble. I think I'd better leave at once. I came to ask if you would drive me past the first town to the village beyond. I must go to Carew to ask my father's advice."

"I will take ye, me lad. But ye need to be more careful of what ye do."

This settled, John went to inform his wife of their departure. He knew he would find her in the bedroom resting. Dorothy was also of Welsh descent. She was tall, very thin, and always ailing, so John did not want to alarm her any more than was necessary. He said, "Dorothy, you must get up, dear, and dress quickly. We are going to town."

She did not ask why. She had learned that John did not like to be questioned, but given ample time he would come through with an explanation. She arose slowly and started dressing.

"Quickly, dear, I said quickly," John said impatiently.

He then went to the only other room in the house and drew out into the middle of the room an old chest that his father had made for him. He started tossing into it the things he thought Dorothy would take if she knew they were leaving never to return. There was nothing of much value to take—some of her fine needlework, bedding, pictures, and a few pieces of china.

When Dorothy finally came from the bedroom she looked about in amazement. "What in the world are you doing?" she cried. Then noticing for the first time the cut on his face, she ran toward him. Softening her voice she exclaimed, "Oh, you are hurt!" He abruptly turned his face so she could not see the wound.

"We are going to leave this place for a while. I think you will feel better living closer to the sea."

"But why should we leave right this minute? You look as if you've been fighting. Come now, tell me, what has happened?" she asked anxiously.

"Well, I did have a little difference with one of the nobility this morning—that young sprig I told you about." John resumed his packing while Dorothy stood watching.

"Please hurry, Dorothy," he said impatiently. "Our good neighbor, Camp Meddleson, will be here soon to drive us to the village. We will take the coach from there. Do not tell anyone where nor why we are going."

"Tell anyone! Tell anyone!" Dorothy cried. "That indeed is a foolish thing to ask, since *I* do not know where or why we are going!" She waited but John did not answer.

"John, why are we leaving here in such disorder?" she persisted.

"Because we must," he replied.

Resignedly, Dorothy returned to the other room, dragged two old valises from under the unmade bed, and began packing.

"God help us," she murmured to herself.

CHAPTER TWO

"One fare to Carew, please."

As John had hoped, the driver did not seem to recognize him as being the same man who had just alighted from his coach and entered the inn a short while before. He was thankful for the darkness.

John stepped up to the door of the stone house and tapped gently. His brothers and sisters would be sleeping, and he did not want to wake them. He held his finger to his lips as his father opened the door and started to exclaim in surprise at seeing his son. His mother was right behind him wondering aloud who would be calling this late at night.

"Oh, Johnny," she cried when she saw his bruised face, "what happened?" As quickly as he could John told them the story. He was anxious to be on his way because he did not want to be found at his parents' house should someone be following him.

His father listened closely, then placed a hand on John's shoulder and said in a very stern voice, "Son, I am proud of your courage. I know how you feel. Time and time again I have had the same impulse when forced to grovel, but you gain nothing by running away from trouble. Go back while there is still time and take your punishment like a man."

"No, Father. I am afraid if I go back it will only lead to more serious trouble."

"I don't think so, John. If you would but apologize to his lordship, you would get only a few lashes. But if you run away like a fugitive and then are caught—son, it might even be death!"

"Death it shall be then, for I will never go back. I have already made up my mind. I shall sail for America."

"America!" his parents exclaimed in astonishment. Then his father spoke again, "Don't be an ass! How much better off will you be there?"

John was disappointed. He had gone straight to his parents hoping for guidance and understanding. He had never expected they would want to send him back to face an angry landlord and possible arrest.

John said, "Mother, do you remember once in Liverpool we attended a meeting held by some men from America? They called themselves Latter Day Saints. There are missionaries from that same church now traveling through Wales. I have attended some of the meetings. They are getting new members to sail to America. A ship leaves from Cardiff within the week. I plan to be on it."

"No, Johnny! Stop and think what you are doing. No good will come from acting so unreasonably. There is no disgrace in taking punishment. Take your father's advice—he knows best." She threw her arms around him, begging, "Please go back, son, and take your punishment like a true subject of the Queen."

John stepped back indignantly. "Mother, don't call me a subject of the Queen. She had nothing to do with my being here on earth, did she? And if I am able to get away, she will have nothing to do with my leaving it!"

"She might have plenty to do with your leaving it if you don't mend your ways!" Mr. Griffiths tried again to reason with his wayward son. "I, too, have heard of that new religion, and what I have heard is not good. The first leader of the Mormons was murdered. There are reports that they are not complying with the laws of the government of the United States. It has been said that a Mormon man can have more than one wife, as in the harems of Egypt."

"Oh, Father, where did you hear that? These are modern times. The United States is made up of many of our own people. They went to America for the same reason that I want to go. They have established laws and principles of right. Their government conforms to certain standards. They would not tolerate injustice."

"And where is Dorothy? She cannot stand the trip to America, and you know it," said his mother.

"I left her in Tenby at White Harte Inn. She will do as I say."

Mr. Griffiths was losing patience. There was but one thing left to do, and that was to demand that his son go back. His eyes were cold as steel when he spoke: "Either you go back and apologize to his lordship... or get out of my house."

"I'm sorry, Father, but I will not alter my plans. I am going to America with the Mormons."

John picked up his cap and went out the door. It was not easy to leave his family this way. As he ran down the road he felt a cold chill run through his body. In the darkness he could see the old watchtower and St. Mary's Church silhouetted against the sky. He knew the vicar there. It was his last chance for help. He hesitated—then went on.

Dorothy realized it would be early morning before John would get back to Tenby, so after the first part of the night she slept poorly, tossing on her pillow until she heard his familiar step at the door. He smiled down on her saying, "See, I told you I would make it back."

John removed his coat and shoes and stretched out on the bed beside her. Dorothy quickly fell asleep again, but John was wide awake. As yet he had not confided his plans to Dorothy. He knew she would be extremely upset over starting out on a venture such as he was planning. He awakened her to talk about it now. Taking hold of her hand he said, "Dorothy, do you know what I have been thinking?"

"No. I am never quite sure what you are thinking, but I don't like a coward's way out."

At the word "coward" he sprang abruptly to his feet.

"Coward! Do you infer that I am a coward?" He did not give Dorothy a chance to answer. "My dear wife, let me inform you here and now that I am not a coward. It never occurred to me that you would think that. I am not afraid to take a flogging. I am afraid the person who tried it would be hurt. We are going to America where we will be rid of all these foolish customs. There I can think for myself without being dictated to. Dorothy, you *must* say you will go."

"All right, John, I will go if it kills me...if that is what you want."

"Come then and get dressed quickly." All the sleep John had had the whole night was on the coach to and from Carew.

"We will go first to the Mormons' meeting so we can see about passage on their boat to America. We must leave here as soon as possible."

"Mormons? What have they to do with us?"

"Darling, do I have to explain every detail when there is so little time? Are we going or not?"

"We are going if that is what you have decided."

"Well, then, make haste."

"My head is whirling so I scarcely can think," she said, but she dressed obediently, put on her wraps, and soon they were leaving the inn.

After they found the building where the Mormons were holding a meeting, Dorothy did not want to enter. It was not her faith, and she hung back. John spoke sharply to her. "Come on! Doesn't my welfare mean anything to you?"

"Of course, but I feel out of place here."

John could see she was nervous, so he placed his arm around her as they entered. A member of the Mormons came forward and offered them a seat.

John wished the sermon would be over so he could get to the business of going to America. But the man talked on and on, comparing Joseph Smith and his followers to the prophet and people of old. Then he described their movement westward from one state to another as they met antagonism. Disagreements and rioting started, and their beloved leader was murdered. Not easily discouraged, the Mormons tried to fight back, but this time the government seemed to turn against them, too, so the entire assembly followed their new leader, Brigham Young, into a territory so far from civilization it was unsettled before them. It was known as the Great Salt Lake Territory, and believed by the U. S. Government to be a vast worthless desert. Brigham Young, however, claimed to have a revelation wherein God directed them to settle there. He was a young and powerful leader, and his followers had great faith in him.

The speaker went on to describe this new settlement.

"Out there vast plains await any man who wishes to claim them, to build himself a home in the name of God and the Latter Day Saints of America. Come one, come all you downtrodden people, we offer you the privilege of earning an honest living, where no man, however great or small, shall have more power than does another."

John was growing more and more interested.

Another of the missionaries came forward and related the healing power of the priesthood, then demonstrated the gift of tongues, while earlier converts walked among the congregation encouraging newcomers to join. John listened intently when special fares to America were offered to those who became members. Passage and meals could be had for only fifty dollars per person. The meeting was closed by the man reading a passage from the Book of Mormon:

It shall come to pass, that the Lord shall give thee rest from thy sorrow and from thy fear and from the hard bondage wherein thou wast made to serve.

Wherefore I say unto you, feast upon the words of Christ, for he will tell you all things to do.

He closed the book and stepped to the edge of the platform, holding one arm above his head for silence. They repeated the Lord's Prayer, after which he added:

"Oh, come forward, my dear brothers and sisters, and join with us. We have faith in the good of mankind in all nations and in all walks of life. And now in the name of God and our great founder Joseph Smith I bless thee one and all. Amen."

John Griffiths got to his feet. He waited a moment for Dorothy, but she made no move to join him. Head held high he walked up the aisle alone.

Before John was converted he felt it was his duty to inform them of his plight. When he reached the altar he did not kneel with the others but waited to confide in the leader. The man listened politely, then placed his hand on John's shoulder, saying, "God said, when they persecute you in one city flee to another. We are proud to have you join with us, my son."

For John it was like a door opening when one is up against a solid wall. Finally he could see his way clear.

CHAPTER THREE

After the meeting, John and Dorothy returned to the inn to wait for the passenger coach which would take them to Cardiff. John was nervous. He went several times to see if it had come. He hoped they would not meet anyone who knew them, and he started in alarm when someone slapped him on the back and said: "Well if it ain't me ol' buddy, Johnny Griffiths."

"Oh, it's you, Pratt. How are you?"

"Yeah, it's me and nobody else. Who did you think it might be? You jumped like you thought it might be the old devil himself!"

"Right now I would rather meet the devil and all his imps than some people I can think of," John replied.

"I hope you don't mean me, Griff."

"No, not you—the law." John knew he could trust Pratt Llanfair.

"Don't tell me you have been commanded to duel the King or someone like that!"

"No, not the King; just one of the Queen's henchmen. And the battle has already been fought. I knocked down an heir to one of the lordships when he called me a bastard and let me have it across the face with his whip."

"Then you are in bad," Pratt said gravely.

"Yes, I'm leaving for America so that I can keep out of trouble."

"You are, eh?"

"But tell me about yourself, Pratt—still in the boating business?"

"I am that, still freighting with my father. Guess I'll stay with the boats—sort of born to it, you know. Are you leaving soon, John, or will you have time to come down to the dock and look at our new outfit? I have a two-masted rigger now."

"Good, glad to hear you are doing so well, Pratt. I would like very much to see your outfit, but I'm waiting now for the passenger coach to Cardiff."

"Cardiff? Say, why not go with me? I have a cargo going over to Gower Peninsula. It would cut your journey in half."

This was indeed a piece of luck for John. On the road from Tenby to Carmarthen was the place officers would most likely be stationed to pick him up. If they went by boat they would pass up that well traveled coach route.

"Pratt, I would be most grateful for the lift. Would you mind if I brought my wife, too?"

"That I surely would. Truly it is a sorry boat for a woman. It is only a freighter, you know, and with poor accommodations. Besides it gets mighty choppy out there in the bay sometimes."

Pratt made all the excuses he could think of, but John replied: "Oh, Dorothy won't mind; she will appreciate the lift. I will go hurry her up."

John left before Pratt could refuse to take a woman on his boat.

It made Dorothy sick just to look at the water, and John knew it but this chance was too good to pass up. Once on Pratt's boat they were safe for at least another day or two.

"Luck is with us, Dorothy—we have a chance to go most of the way to Cardiff on one of Llanfair's boats," John announced, pushing her toward the door. There was no time for discussion for Pratt was waiting for them.

Just then there came a rapping on the door.

"John, it's me, Pratt. Sorry old boy, but I'll have to shove off without you. We have to go with the tide, you know, and I—well, there is no time to wait."

John threw open the door and almost knocked Pratt down as he shoved the valises out into the hallway.

"Give me a lift with our valises, will ye? We're ready."

"How nice of you, Mr. Llanfair," Dorothy said as she grabbed up her shawl and basket and hurried after them.

John didn't give Pratt another chance to argue them out of going. He hurried outside and hailed a carriage to take them down to the harbor.

The pier was built out away from the shore and during low tide the water was very shallow. Llanfair's boat was anchored out in the bay. He asked Dorothy to wait on the pier. Then he went ahead in a skiff he had moored there. He wanted to prepare the crew for the presence of a woman on board.

John waited on shore with Dorothy. Soon after Pratt boarded the freighter they could see there was much activity aboard; evidently Pratt had given orders to clean out below. They accomplished this by heaving the debris overboard. Seagulls came in large numbers, circling over the boat, squawking and flapping their wings and diving down to devour the refuse.

Finally Pratt came back and they were rowed out to the freighter.

"My, but you have lots of seafowl around you!" Dorothy exclaimed as she pointed to the gulls.

As they left Tenby the rugged coastline with its high cliffs was very impressive. Now and then a patch of green and a farmhouse showed up. Even in their circumstances they could not but enjoy the beauty of it. Dorothy gazed at it long and hard so she would never forget it.

At last they arrived at the port, where they pulled into the dock just long enough for Dorothy and John to leave the boat. Then Pratt would go on to the smelter with his cargo. John thanked him warmly for the lift across the bay. It was now too late to journey farther; already it was turning dusk.

Fortunately a passenger coach was leaving there for Cardiff early next morning. It would approach the city from a different route than if they had come from Pembrokeshire. This John hoped would help them avoid any who might be watching for them.

Dorothy was very tired, and went right to bed when they found lodging at a small "bed and breakfast" inn. But it was hard for either of them to fall asleep because of what the next day might bring.

At noon on the day they reached Cardiff, the driver stopped for refreshments and change of horses at a small hamlet. He drew the carriage to a stop at a wayside pub. There were five other passengers, and all were anxious to alight and stretch their weary limbs.

After everyone else was out Dorothy said to John, "Let us take our basket and go on yonder hill to eat lunch." She pointed to a small knoll just above the pub. They climbed up to where they could see the waters of Bristol Channel shimmering in the distance.

Dorothy had packed a basket of food so they would not have to enter the pubs along the way to eat as did the other passengers. She did it not only for the sake of her husband's safety but to save their meager funds. John spread out the blanket and Dorothy took out the lunch, such as it was: crackers and cheese and tea cakes.

John ate fast and heartily, then stretched himself full length onto the ledge, face on his folded arms. It felt good to stretch out after being cramped in the carriage for so long.

Dorothy ate scarcely any food at all. She was so afraid of what might take place next. Suddenly she was alerted by the sound of children's voices and the sharp barking of a dog. Soon three children and their pet came into sight from behind the ledge. A girl of about twelve, a younger boy, and a tiny little girl all stopped short on seeing John and Dorothy.

"Do not be afraid," Dorothy said kindly. "We are eating our lunch here. Would you like to feed the scraps to your dog?"

They moved forward and stood while Dorothy tossed small pieces of her cracker to the dog. The children laughed while he scampered after them. John did not look up, so Dorothy supposed he had fallen asleep.

Hearing a commotion below, Dorothy turned quickly to look. She trembled with fear when she saw three officers alight from their horses and enter the inn. They had not seemed to look in their direction, yet Dorothy was so frightened she scarcely knew what to do. It would be impossible to hide with the children there. Besides, if they were looking for John, they would check with the driver at the inn.

If only John would stay down, he would not be visible from the road below. Dorothy decided not to arouse him. She kept up a conversation with the children so they would not leave, believing they would be their best shield from the law.

Presently the officers came out of the pub. Two of them mounted their horses and rode away but the other, leading his mount, walked toward them.

Dorothy pressed her hands together till her fingernails cut into her flesh. Then she began tossing whole tea cakes to the dog feigning merriment with loud bursts of nearly hysterical laughter.

The scene apparently looked innocent enough to the officer, for he did not come closer but called out to them: "Have you seen a stranger here about? I am looking for a fugitive of the law."

CHAPTER FOUR

Dorothy was so stunned she was unable to make a sound. She could see the muscles in John's shoulders tense, so she knew he was not asleep. She prayed that God would spare her the sight of her husband being shot down by this lawman. She knew John would never be apprehended without a fight. It seemed like an eternity to her, but it was only a few moments before the oldest child answered the officer: "Oh, no sir, there is only just us here," she said cheerfully, taking in everyone with a sweep of her hand. "We are having fun," she added.

The officer hesitated, then mounted his horse and rode away to catch up with the others, evidently satisfied they had been just some villagers picnicking with their children.

Dorothy could feel the blood slowly coming back into her face and her heartbeat slowing. The sun was gone, and she began shivering.

"Come, John, quick. I am so cold. Will you hurry to the coach and get my shawl?"

It was soon time to resume their journey. They traveled far into the night to reach Cardiff, and the heavy black shawl Dorothy wore was not sufficient to protect her from the chilling winds and cold night air. By the time they reached the suburbs of the city where they left the coach, Dorothy had contracted a severe cold.

John searched until he found a small, reasonably priced room that was clean.

He insisted that Dorothy go to bed at once. He helped her to get settled, then went to a corner shop where he purchased some tea which he hoped would warm her.

All through the night Dorothy shivered and coughed. John was up several times to reheat the tea—it was all he had to relieve her. He was glad when daylight came.

"Last night I was so anxious to see Cardiff," Dorothy said, "but now I am so sick and tired I don't even want to get up."

"You will see it in time. It is best for you to rest this morning while I go down to the docks. If I was given the right information in Tenby there isn't much time before our boat sails."

John was so excited he ran most of the way to the wharf. The ship—*his* ship—was not as new or as big as some, but it was beautiful to behold. Even now its sails were being let out, shining pure white in the sun. Activity on board indicated that sailing time was not far off. There were many ships in port, and John had a hard time finding someone who knew anything about the small vessel anchored out from the dock. He did not want to go to the office where he might be asked his name. At last a man working on the dock told him the ship would be anchored at the wharf the following morning, which indicated it would be leaving within the week.

After watching the boats for a while John went back to the lodging house. Dorothy was still in bed. John was quite disturbed by her condition and wanted to call a doctor, but Dorothy would not hear of it. They had very little money, and she did not want to land in America without means of survival.

Dorothy did not tell John, but she noticed that in the afternoons her face felt flushed and her heart would suddenly beat fast, then slowly—so slowly it seemed it would stop. Respiration was difficult and painful. Dorothy feared consumption, but she was determined to keep this from John. She insisted she would be able to leave when the boat sailed.

John believed that once Dorothy was on the boat and sure they were out of danger she would relax and feel better. It seemed to him she had been ailing, in one way or another, ever since they had been married. Anything that upset her would bring on a headache or a "spell." Therefore he was not unduly concerned.

He went several times a day to the wharf and to the inn where the Mormons gathered. Activity aboard the ship was increasing. Not only were the old sails being mended but new ones were coming on board, plus bolts of canvas and coils of rigging—in short, everything indicated that preparations were coming to a close. Notice was given at the inn, where the ship's company and the Mormons were staying, that they must be on board before night. There was no telling exactly when the vessel would sail, as they must go with the tide and wind.

After getting their luggage ready, John helped Dorothy to dress, but when the time came to put on her wraps she collapsed, and John had to help her back to bed. She was obviously unable to travel.

John had never known such a disappointment as when he watched the ship sail away without him. His hopes were shattered. It grieved Dorothy to see John so completely broken.

After months of nursing she was at last able to be up part of each day. The summer had been kind to her. John had insisted that she have plenty of milk and butter and other foods she needed to regain her strength. He had found work at a smelter but spent very little on himself, saving like a miser for the voyage to America he was still determined to make.

Now that they had ceased to worry quite so much about the law, Dorothy suggested he give up the notion of going to America, but John would not listen. One day he arrived home from work earlier than usual, acting more cheerful than he had for a long time. Each day thereafter he came home bringing little packages; one day a pocket knife, the next day a compass and several pairs of warm stockings for Dorothy. She began to wonder at his behavior. Then there came the day that he returned home and announced he had quit his job.

"You might as well come out with it, John—it's obvious you are keeping something from me," Dorothy said.

"Yes, my dear, I do have something to tell you. I have known for several days now, but I kept it from you so you would not have time to dwell on it and arouse one of your spells."

"Now, don't be silly. I don't 'arouse' those spells. I don't want to be ill."

"I know that, dear, but you are inclined to worry about little things, and I want you to be strong and well right now. I have learned there is another contingent of Mormons leaving right after the New Year."

"Tomorrow is New Year's Day," Dorothy said.

"Yes, I know, and the next day we will go aboard the ship. I ran into those missionaries we met in Tenby at the meeting where I joined the church. They are going home on this boat, so it will be like sailing with friends."

"John... must we go?"

"I am compelled to go. When the country in which I was born refuses to allow me to be free, then I must live in a country which does," John declared.

"How will you earn a livelihood there?" she asked.

"As I have here—by my hands. The difference is, I will not be looked down upon because of it."

"Have you thought, John, that it is winter?"

"It will be coming spring when we arrive."

Dorothy laid down her needle but did not speak or get up.

She bestirred herself as little as possible, as it often brought on a coughing spell. She knew John's mind was made up. There was no use arguing.

On a bitterly cold day in January, 1851, they set sail for America.

John helped Dorothy get into her warmest clothes, praying she would not collapse. He wrapped her in her big black shawl so she wouldn't get cold on the way to the ship. He even carried her out to where a cab waited. He had taken every measure possible to save her strength, yet in the short distance to the ship she had more than one coughing spell. John was extremely upset when he saw her wipe a fleck of blood from her lips, but he felt they could not turn back again. At the ship Dorothy tried to walk unaided, but her legs gave out and John was forced to carry her up the long gangplank. Other passengers pushed forward, and one young lady was shoved into John's path. After coldly staring at her John lowered his head and stepped around. He carried Dorothy straight to their cabin and laid her gently on the bunk. She held her arms tightly around his neck and said, "John, dear, you are so good to me. I am sorry I ever doubted your judgment. Please forgive me. I am sure we will have a jolly time. I hope I feel better tomorrow."

Several times during her conversation Dorothy had to pause to cough. Her sentences were short and jerky. John released her arms from around his neck and gently pulled the covers up around her.

"Darling, I know you will. We have a long life ahead of us. When we walk off this ship we will be able to build a home on our own land. Try to think about that. Try and rest now while I fetch the rest of our luggage."

She looked so pale he stood with his hand on the door, undecided if he should leave her or not.

On deck a sharp wind had come up, and the sailors were working with all speed to take advantage of it. One could feel the impact as the wind caught in the main topsail. The ship had to sail out of Bristol Bay on high tide because at low tide the water was very shallow.

The captain stood on the bridge directing his crew, shouting his orders so as to be heard above the turmoil. Waves were washing against the sides of the ship and slashing against the pier. Seabirds were screeching and fighting over scraps of garbage floating on the water. John was thrilled by it all. He stood bareheaded, looking up at the sky then down at the water which was becoming choppy with the wind and the turning of the tide. He thought sadly of Dorothy who was not well enough to be out here. She had been cheated of her youth because of ill health.

John felt like staying on deck and joining in the fun. Instead he went back to the cabin, where he found Dorothy had fallen asleep. He noticed that her face was flushed. He felt lonely as he sat there listening to the sound of her breathing. After an hour or so he went out again. It was harder to walk as the movement of the ship increased. When he reached the deck he saw Cardiff in the distance.

Although John had wanted to leave his homeland, now that he actually was on the way he had a strange feeling. Wales was fast fading from his sight. It was the flag flying that touched him most—a flag honored the world over. John was glad he had escaped without getting into more serious trouble. He did not want to dishonor his country.

When he got back to the cabin Dorothy was worse. He was suddenly filled with guilt. He had not been willing to give up another chance to go to America because of her health. If anything happened to Dorothy now, he felt it would be his fault. He was sorry he had not given more consideration to her health, but it was too late to turn back now.

John's sleep was interrupted many times that night by Dorothy's cough and heavy breathing. Daybreak found him tired and worn. Her condition deteriorated still further, and shortly John rushed out in search of the doctor.

CHAPTER FIVE

Most of the passengers on the ship were associated with the Mormons. Among those who were not were a Welsh blacksmith, Daniel Thomas, and his family. Thomas had heard that it would be easy for a man of his trade to make a living in America. He was bound for the States not for religious freedom or the newly found gold fields in California, but for an easier and better life.

His family consisted of a young wife and two small children as well as three older children by his first wife. His eldest daughter Mary was twenty-two; his son Tommy was sixteen; and little Hannah was ten. His first wife had died at Hannah's birth and Sally James, who had come to care for the mother, had stayed on to nurse the ailing child. She filled the mother's place so completely that after a few years Daniel knew he could not get along without her and asked her to be his wife. She quickly consented, having loved him for a long time. Also traveling with the Thomases was Sally's sister, Letticia.

On that first morning away from land Mary Thomas arose and dressed carefully. As she passed her father's cabin she poked her head in long enough to say she would meet the rest of the family in the dining room. Mary wanted to go by herself, thinking she might meet the young man whom she had seen carrying an older woman. She observed everyone that entered for breakfast—and for lunch and dinner—but the man did not appear. She asked her father, "Does everyone eat in the dining room?"

"The crew members don't, and I understand that on some ships there is a section on a lower deck where passengers pay less and furnish their own meals. Why do you ask?"

"Oh, I just wondered. There seems to be more people on the ship than come to the dining room."

"Well, we do not all eat at the same time."

Of course, that explains his absence, Mary thought. Surely a man and woman who arrived in a carriage would not be traveling steerage.

When Sally heard that a very ill passenger was aboard she wanted to offer assistance. She asked a steward the location of the sick person's cabin and was told that the woman's husband was caring for her and had said he didn't need assistance. Sally told Mary about this, and Mary knew it must be the woman she had seen being carried aboard. The woman must have appeared old because of her illness.

The winter sun soon merged into darkness. Everyone was tired after the first day at sea. Mr. Thomas retired early. Letticia went to bed battling seasickness. Mary, left to herself, began to wonder what her brother was doing. She decided to search for him. He would be somewhere out on deck.

A light wind was blowing steadily, and the ship was making good progress. The moon was full but could be seen only intermittently through the clouds. Mary circled the deck without catching sight of Tommy and had just decided to go below again when suddenly a steward opened the door of a room directly in front of her. She caught a glimpse of a man kneeling at the bedside of a woman.

The ship's doctor hurried past her and went into the room shutting the door behind him. Mary stood staring at the door, caught up in the drama of the situation. Suddenly the door burst open and the young man emerged. He leaned against the lifeboat very close to Mary, lowered his head to his arms, and burst into sobs.

Suddenly a soft, warm hand touched his. "She would not want you to give up now, would she?"

He looked up and saw that she was the same girl who had been pushed in his way when he had carried Dorothy aboard. Once again she had witnessed him in an embarrassing situation.

"I beg your pardon, miss; I did not see you here," he said stiffly.

"Oh, please forgive me," Mary said quickly. "I could not keep from speaking to you in your sorrow. I came here looking for my brother. If there is nothing I can do to help you, I will go now."

Mary felt her face grow warm and was thankful that the darkness hid her blushes. Not only had she invited a conversation with a strange man but had taken hold of his hand.

"My wife was ill when we came aboard. It was my fault that we came. She was very frail and could endure little exertion, but I did not realize—or perhaps I did not want to realize—that her condition was so serious," he explained.

The door of the stateroom was opened. The doctor and a seaman were wrapping the body for burial at sea. He clutched her hand until it hurt. She felt it would be unkind to leave him now, so Mary waited. Finally John seemed to get a grip on himself. "I am terribly sorry, miss, that I thrust my grief upon you. I feel better now. Thank you so much."

"I must go now," Mary said softly.

"Of course," he replied, after pausing a moment as if he wished to say more. He lightly touched her arm as he led her back to the lighted deck.

"My name is John Griffiths. I am traveling to the Great Salt Lake country with the Mormons. We had planned to make a home there. What is your name, miss?"

"Mary Thomas," she replied.

He bowed low and said, "Good night, Miss Thomas." Then he vanished into the night.

Because Dorothy had died of consumption and lung hemorrhage, John was ordered to take his few belongings and move to other quarters.

Everyone on board seemed to be content except John. He held himself aloof from other passengers. He often sat for hours at a time on top of the cases of cargo that were piled high on the prow of the ship, thinking remorsefully of the past.

One day while he was thus engaged he was surprised to see the little Thomas girl climbing up the cases above him, pulling a little boy up behind her. The boy was trying to jerk away from her and in the tussle they both lost their footing and came rolling down almost on top of him. On seeing John, they quickly got to their feet and ran off again down the other side, leaving their older sister Mary, who was calling them to come back, to apologize for their bad behavior.

John quickly got to his feet and dusted his neat but threadbare coat. "It is pleasant up here," he said. "One can get away from all mortal souls. Won't you sit down and enjoy the solitude with me?"

He looked lonely, she thought. He deliberately secluded himself from the other young people and their merrymaking.

One would think he would seek companionship now of all times, throught Mary, and she replied sharply, "I hope you have not lost faith in yourself again."

"No, definitely not. I have learned some things—especially never to lose faith in one's self or God."

Mary wanted to stay and talk, but she knew she must return to the deck. Her father was very strict, and he would not approve of her being up there alone with a stranger. John took the cap he had been holding in his hand and dusted off the canvas covering of one of the boxes, then pointed for Mary to sit down on it, but she had already started to climb down.

"I must find those little ones," she said. "They get into a great deal of mischief."

Later that day Mary saw John standing on the deck. She hurried to her cabin and changed her dress. A cold wind was blowing, but Mary did not want to cover up her pretty dress, so she went without a wrap toward where John was standing. He glanced casually in her direction, then very gallantly tipped his cap. For a moment his face lit up with pleasure, and he gave her a rare smile. Mary quickened her step, but before she could reach his side, he had turned his gaze back to the sea. It was obviously a rebuff. Mary was confused and hurt. What had caused the sudden change in John? Could he not see she had sought him out? Had he thought her to be presumptuous or immodest? She turned back to her cabin with tears in her eyes.

CHAPTER SIX

Mary was finding it impossible to fall asleep. The woodwork and fittings groaned and squeaked, the yellow sea lamp rocked back and forth, and her imagination ran on and on. Tommy had not yet retired, and she began to wish she had gone for a stroll with him.

Finally she decided to get up and dress and go for a walk after all. She wrapped a shawl about her and went out on deck. The cold wind felt good on her face. Perhaps I will run into Tom out here, she thought.

Mary found it exciting being on deck at night after most of the passengers had gone to bed. She had not intended to wander so far from her cabin, but she was at the stern of the ship before she realized it. She had gone directly to the place where John Griffiths was usually found. Remembering what had taken place the last time she sought him out, she felt afraid to go any farther and had just turned to hurry away when someone took hold of her and held her back. She jerked free and started to run, but before she could take two steps a man grabbed her again. Her heart seemed to come up into her throat because she recognized the seaman who had been staring at her and pestering her with silly remarks ever since she came aboard.

He was a big, husky fellow, but Mary felt more indignation than fear. Again she pulled away. "Let me go!" she demanded.

Perhaps the man meant no harm, but Mary never knew what he had in mind for just then John Griffiths stepped out of the shadows. He said sharply to the seaman: "I will escort Miss Thomas back to her cabin, sir."

The fellow scuttled away without answering. He knew this kind of conduct could cause him trouble if it were reported to the captain.

Mary, now trembling with fright, was glad that John had come to her rescue. "Oh, thank you," she said feebly. Then she felt she should explain why she was out on deck at this hour of the night. "I came out for a breath of air. I could not sleep."

"Nor could I," John said. "I really was hoping I might find you. I don't believe I ever thanked you properly for being so understanding and kind to me the night my wife died. I had not a relative or close friend to turn to."

Mary was silent so long that he wondered whether she had heard him. She wanted to say how happy she was that he had found her. Instead she said, "I like to help people if they appreciate it."

"Appreciate it! My dear girl, had it not been for you, I might have flung myself overboard. You see, I forced my wife to come on this voyage though she was very ill. She did not let me know *how* ill until we were on the ship. But I should have known—anyone should have recognized the seriousness of her coughing." John paused a moment, then went on: "In fact, I am so deeply grateful to you that I have not been able to keep it from my mind. Yet, I could not bring myself to speak to you of it. In some way our meeting seemed like something holy. Mere words could not do it justice. I hope you understand."

"I do understand, now," Mary said. "I had thought that you did not care to know me."

"Miss Thomas! There are moments when the soul is kneeling, no matter what the attitude of the body might be!" John said, quoting Victor Hugo.

They stepped close to the rail of the ship as a big wave reared up between the ship and the western horizon. They stood side by side, enjoying the motion of the ship as it topped wave after wave.

John remarked, "My life has been somewhat like those waves— down low, then riding on top of the crest. That is how I feel now, with you standing here beside me. I don't have much hope, but to know we are friends means a great deal."

Mary was unable to put her feelings into words, so she said nothing. She felt like crying, yet she was filled with joy. She thought even if they were parted and traveled separate roads through life, there would ever linger the memory of this night.

A strong wind came up and thickened the spray falling on deck. John drew Mary's shawl more securely around her shoulders and let his hand rest there. He was not a particularly sociable man, but he felt like talking to Mary. She seemed lovelier than anyone he had ever known.

The loneliness John endured had become almost unbearable, but suddenly he felt he could accept the hardships, could excuse and pardon them all, if fate would grant him this girl's love. Yet, because of his wife's recent death, he could not ask for it. Mary might think less of him if he did. Others certainly would look askance. Amid the roar of the wind and the crash of the water, conversation was almost impossible.

The captain passed by, and Mary shouted at him, "It's getting a bit rough, eh, Captain?"

He smiled but did not answer. Perhaps he did not understand her, or perhaps he did not pay much attention to the familiar roar of the ocean and the continual tossing of the ship—or perhaps he did not consider this a rough sea, having experienced many worse.

The ship began to roll more, and sailors appeared. Some made their way up the masts, taking in sails and changing the course a little to the southward. The crewmen were laughing, cursing, and singing as they went about their tasks.

John walked Mary back to her stateroom. On the way he invited her to attend the meetings of the Latter Day Saints, some of which he had the pleasure of conducting.

"I notice your father is not one of us," he said.

"No, Father is a very devout Christian but not a Mormon."

"I wasn't before, either, but I found the teachings are more to my way of thinking than any other religion I know about. I hope you don't mind that I am a Mormon."

"Oh, no, I don't. Father has taught us that everyone should have a right to his own beliefs."

"Do you think you could be a Mormon?"

"I don't know. Father decides those things for the family."

"I see."

"Would it please you if I came to the meetings?"

"I would . . . it would please me very much."

She watched his face. He seemed to have something he wanted to say. She waited for his next words.

"It is a strange thing—ever since we first met, in fact ever since I first set eyes on you, the day I came aboard, I have felt drawn toward you. And since the night you gave me courage, after I had lost mine, I have sensed an understanding between us. All our meetings have appeared to be preordained. It is a strange feeling. Are you aware of it also?"

"Yes, I am. But I had no idea you shared my feelings," Mary replied.

At this particular moment the middle-aged couple who had a stateroom adjacent to that of the Thomases strolled past. They stopped to say good-night, and the woman added, "We are glad you are getting over your bereavement, Mr. Griffiths."

Not only the words but the tone she used made John feel she was criticizing his behavior. Mary noticed the faint creases about his eyes and mouth deepen, and she knew he was disturbed.

"Pay them no heed. I know you will ever hold in your heart the memory of your wife. But only the past belongs to her. The future is yours," she said after the couple had gone on.

"Ours," he corrected, then added, "Whatever your opinion, there can be no doubt of that of your friends."

He was anxious to amend the impression the people had received. He also felt he should not have spoken to Mary as he had, from the depths of his soul. He would have to be careful to maintain a more reserved manner. He called out to the couple who were just ahead.

"Would you mind waiting for Miss Thomas? I was escorting her back to her cabin; but since you are going her way, I will bid you all good-night here."

John turned sharply and departed. He hoped this would allay any presumptuous ideas the pair might have. And he hoped that Mary would understand, too, and keep her distance.

Later that night, the captain was thrown from his bunk by a terrific jolt. He threw on his clothes and burst from his quarters calling for his mate and crew. Everyone on the ship had been awakened by the terrific impact.

The mate came rushing down the corridor, dressing as he came. He shouted to the captain, "What can it be, sir?"

The captain did not answer. He was preparing to go on deck as quickly as he could.

"We are too far out to sea—we could not have struck land," continued the mate.

The captain, running past, still did not answer. He was much too concerned to answer idle questions. He had never known such a terrific jolt to occur, unless caused by a blast inside or something they struck. He believed neither had happened.

The mate was still dogging his heels. "Maybe we hit another ship, sir."

Clinging to the door, the captain peered out into the darkness. It was the dead of night and so black he could not see his hand before him. A blanket of spray slapped him in the face. The ship was rolling so they could not stand erect. Clinging to the door, he made his way outside where horror filled his soul. The gale was stronger than anything he had ever experienced before. The jolt had been caused by the wind's sudden catching of the sails. The waves were rolling higher than the masts and looked as if they would break over them at any moment.

The captain cried out in fear, "My God, a hurricane has caught us in full sail!"

CHAPTER SEVEN

The ship labored heavily to rise again out of the sea. As the wind increased, the waves grew higher. All crew members were now on deck, clinging to whatever object they could to reach their stations. Even the least experienced realized that only their speed could save the ship from destruction.

"Let down the anchor and reduce the sails. There is no time to untie the knots—cut them with your knives. Up the masts, me lads, and double quick. The wrath of God is upon us!"

That they all knew, but just how they could cling to the masts and make fast the sails, they did not know. Still they went, not a one questioning his safety.

The gale was now blowing over seventy miles an hour and increasing with every blast. Sails were being ripped to pieces. At times the torn ends of the canvas snapping in the wind sounded like pistol shots ringing out across the water.

The captain called for the second mate. "Quillish, take charge of the passengers and order them below. Use force if necessary, but keep them off this deck. Provide as many of them as you can with life belts in readiness to leave the ship if necessary."

Before Quillish could stop them, several men pushed open a door against the wind. It was torn from its hinges and blown away like a piece of kindling.

Quillish found the salon filled with uproar and confusion. Most of the passengers had gathered there. Some were crying and screaming, while others were struck dumb with fright. The braver ones were giving what aid and comfort they could, but most all were rendered helpless with seasickness from the tossing of the ship. The storm continued, hour after hour. The salon was filled with groans and prayers and the reek of vomitus. Some of the Mormons were shouting out prayers for others. Some were asking deliverance for themselves. Above all this chaos rose the sound of wind and sea.

But there were some in the salon who kept their heads. One was John Griffiths. Another was young Tommy Thomas from Carmarthanshire. The second mate knew the captain was desperately in need of brave men to help save the ship. On noticing their courage he ordered those men who were able to go out and aid the captain, cautioning them to watch their step lest they be washed overboard.

Tommy and John had no more than spoken to each other before this night, but as they ventured out into the storm there was a feeling of comradeship between them. The spray blinded them, and when they opened their mouths to speak their lungs were forced full of air. The wind and water washing over the deck threw them off their feet more than once as they searched in the darkness for something to grasp.

The ship was now traveling at a terrific speed. Before the crew could reduce its sails the anchor was dragging. Above the roar the captain heard the quartermaster calling frantically for help.

"Captain, I can no longer hold the ship to—the helm is turning in my hands! For God's sake, someone, help me!"

There was no time to send below for help, and every man out there was needed at his post, so the captain started to go himself to aid the quartermaster. On the way he stumbled over John and Tommy. He grabbed them and pushed them along until they could regain their footing. It took able-bodied seamen to stand erect in this gale.

The captain shouted to them: "Put your strength to the helm, me lads; we must keep her straight. No power on earth can save us if once she goes broadside."

It took the combined strength of John and Tommy and the quartermaster at the helm to keep the ship from going lopsided. The sails that were not torn to shreds had either been cut loose or taken up, and they were running now with bare masts.

At break of day, they again tried to weigh anchor, but the crew was so exhausted that those passengers who were able were forced to give a hand.

Those remaining below were worried that their loved ones who had gone to aid the crew might have met with disaster. Mary's heart was torn with anxiety over her brother. She also had another fear. Where was John Griffiths? He had gone out there, too. Deep in her heart she was sure she loved him. Mary sat there with her arms around her little sister, Hannah. She could hardly keep from dashing out into the storm to find the man she loved. She would be willing to work beside him to help save all their lives. She knew she was stronger than some who had gone out there in the storm to do what they could to help. Her own father was worn out from seasickness and worry over his family. He cursed himself again and again for bringing them on this dangerous voyage.

As the day wore on, the storm seemed to grow worse, and the captain feared destruction was imminent. Once the wind blew with such velocity he was afraid he would have to cut away the foremast to bring the ship to.

John and Tommy had stayed at their post so long that their bodies as well as their minds were numb. John began to fear that Tommy would collapse, and if he did, they would not be able to hold the helm. Each time the ship rose on a wave he wondered if it would be the last. Then two men arrived, sent by the captain to relieve the pair at the helm. Tommy was so exhausted he lay down where he was. John made his way below. He believed certain death was in store for all on the ship and wanted to spend his last moments near the one he loved. For the moment he forgot his obligation to the memory of his wife. He did not even consider what Mary would think, nor what her family would think. His thoughts were only of her and of his desire that they perish together.

When Mary saw John come into the salon, she ran to him crying, "Where is Tommy? What has become of him?"

"He is still safe, my darling," he replied tenderly.

Losing her bravery when there was someone stronger to lean on, Mary began sobbing.

"What shall we do, John? What *shall* we do?"

He took Mary in his arms and pressed her hard against his heart. No words of love passed between them; only the nearness of death was in their minds. Expecting these moments to be the last, John, looking upward, prayed as he had never prayed before. Others joined in the prayer, until with one voice they beseeched God for deliverance.

As the day wore on, the storm moderated and the sea grew calmer, but the thing that saved them appeared to be an act of God—a shift in the wind that now beat down the sea.

Tommy entered the salon, and Mary left John to meet her brother. The tossing of the ship diminished, and people began getting over their sickness and fear. Now, while all the Thomases were clinging to Tommy, John excused himself and made his way out.

As soon as the captain was sure the storm was abating

and his presence was no longer needed at his post, he hurried to his quarters and sent for the ship's doctor, who also had been working all night long.

"What are the casualties?"

"Astonishing as it may seem, Captain, there are no deaths... and only one broken leg. Most everyone has bruises and lacerations. Some seasickness prevails, but nothing more serious. There was some fainting and the like among the women."

"Thank you, doctor. Send Quillish in, will you?"

Quillish's hair was snarled and uncombed, his clothes in a state of disorder. He was now working on his third shift and about to collapse.

"Go to your quarters and return looking like an officer," the captain ordered when he saw his mate.

When Quillish returned the captain also had changed to a fresh uniform and was well groomed, as a captain should be.

"Quillish, as soon as you have eaten, see about getting some of the crew on deck to separate the yards from the junk fastened to them, and save all the cordage and canvas that can be used again. Make sure all loose crates are secured."

"Aye, aye, Captain!"

A short time later the captain appeared at his station on the quarterdeck, immaculate in appearance although his body ached. The only outward sign of his ordeal was a slight hoarseness. Some of the strength of the sea seemed to be reflected in him as he stood there scanning the havoc on deck. He was proud of his ship; it had, with the help of God, weathered a mighty storm.

The next day John Griffiths stopped by the Thomases' quarters to inquire after Tommy. Mary gave him a chilling glance when he had the audacity to ask her father, in her presence, how his daughters were. After the embrace they had shared the day before, why did he not come to her? Mr. Thomas thanked him for leading them in prayer and for helping them to come safely through the storm.

John looked across at Mary. Her cheeks were flushed and her eyes revealed anger and indignation. He knew he must offer her an explanation for his actions... but not here. He shook hands with Mr. Thomas, then reached toward Mary, pressing her hand lightly. He could see the light come into her face, but knew that for a while yet he must shut his heart against their love for each other.

CHAPTER EIGHT

New Orleans was one hundred miles up the Mississippi River, so it was some time after sighting land until the ship's passengers felt the firmness of earth under their feet. As the river wound around the many curves and bends up from the Gulf of Mexico they watched eagerly for the city to appear. At last they sighted it on the east bank of the river.

All the Thomases were on deck, taking in the sights. Mr. Thomas pointed out a steamboat, like they would continue their journey on after leaving New Orleans. Even Mary had come out on deck to watch the landing and to give John one more chance to redeem himself. Once off the boat she knew they would never meet again. But he did not come to bid her farewell.

It seemed hours before the ship finally came to a standstill and the passengers were allowed to disembark. It was a beautiful, warm day—a pleasant contrast to the cold weather they had left behind in Wales. But Mary left the ship with a heavy heart.

John was ashamed of himself for not offering to help the Thomases from the boat. He knew he should have gone to Mary, but he could not. He kept thinking of Dorothy and how they had pictured the occasion when they would land, free people, on American soil. Somehow he could not bring himself to leave the ship with some other woman. So, bound by his conscience to pay this last tribute to her, he walked from the ship alone.

The Thomases obtained passage to the St. Charles Hotel in a horse-drawn coach. Inside the hotel Mary walked over to an open window and stood gazing out. The sun was shining, and the garden was filled with sweet scented flowers, but Mary was not touched by it. She had been deeply hurt by John's obvious intention to have nothing further to do with her. Then she sensed someone's presence beside her, and turned to see none other than the man she loved.

"Why did you come here?" she blurted.

"Because I knew I would find you here."

"Don't you assume a great deal, Mr. Griffiths?"

"On the contrary. I knew you would be here before you knew it yourself."

"But how could you have known that?"

"I recommended this hotel to your father, since it was where I would be staying."

John looked happy and carefree and kept smiling at her. It seemed to Mary that this was a different John than the one she had known on the ship.

"If you wanted us to be friends, then why did you treat me so coldly on the boat?"

"Need you ask? It would not have been proper of one so recently bereaved. But let us not think of the past, my dear; it is time to plan for the future." Mary could only smile for joy.

They remained but a few days in New Orleans. Mary wanted to leave at the same time John did. Mr. Thomas and Sally were anxious to be out of the South, not only because they did not like to see the abuse of Negroes but also because of the yellow fever. Nearly one thousand persons had been stricken with it that year. So John, the Thomas family, and the Mormons were soon on their way up the Mississippi River to St. Louis. The journey would take five days.

On the riverboat Mr. Thomas began to make plans for the future. He asked many questions of the men he met who had been west of the Mississippi. They all told him that Council Bluffs was an ideal place to set up a blacksmith shop, but they did not all agree on how to get there. Some said overland, but most said it was best to go by boat.

"Mama, I have changed our plans," he told Sally. "I hear we can leave this boat at St. Louis and go from there on a barge up the Missouri River to Council Bluffs. It will, no doubt, be more costly, but it is far less hazardous, so they tell me, than going cross-country in the wagons with the Mormons. What do you think?"

"Yes, because of the children I think it would be better."

Mary was upset by the news. She hated the thought of being separated from John. The Mormons were going on up the Mississippi River to a Mormon settlement where they would join with others waiting there to travel via wagon train to the Great Salt Lake country.

Mary had been hoping that her father would become converted to the faith of the Latter Day Saints and go on to Salt Lake with them, but Mr. Thomas was firm in his beliefs. There were some things about the Mormons he could not accept.

One thing he objected to was that they were so anxious for new members they would permit almost anyone to travel with them. Some who had been converted in New Orleans did not appear trustworthy to Mr. Thomas.

There was much loose talk on the boat about the Mormons. John overheard things that both astonished and displeased him. Some passengers who had come aboard at Memphis were Missourians. They had a peculiar way of speaking, John thought, and as soon as they were on the boat they began insulting the Mormons. John heard them say that the Mormons had been run out of every state across the country because of their illicit way of living. He overheard two men bragging about having burned the homes and barns of Mormons at Nauvoo and stolen their stock.

John had been about to ask Mr. Thomas if he could marry his daughter and take her with him to the Salt Lake country, but this conversation made him reconsider. He was going in search of the Mormon missionaries to ask their opinion when he met Mary, who had some more upsetting news for him.

"Oh, John, Father has just told me we are going to leave the boat at St. Louis!"

"Why? What is the matter?"

"Nothing, but he has decided to go with some others up the Missouri River on a flatboat to Council Bluffs. He says it is safer."

"I see. Some do say that is a better way to travel."

John wanted desperately to ask her to go on with him, regardless of her father's plans. He wanted to ask her to continue the journey to Salt Lake as his wife. He knew that she expected him to, but under the circumstances he could not. He would not selfishly endanger her life.

John took Mary's hand and held it while he said, "Darling, please trust me. Something has come up that I must see the Mormons about. My plans for the future depend on this. I will see you later, maybe in an hour or so. Meet me here. I'll not be longer than I have to." He left her abruptly.

When John questioned the Mormons they admitted their members had been subjected to ill treatment in nearly all the states in which they had tried to settle, but the only real trouble they encountered was in Missouri and Illinois. They declared, however, that it was not because of any illicit living but because the direct revelations they received from God had enabled them to progress further than some people could understand.

John returned to where Mary was waiting for him. He sought for the right words to say. "Mary, I do not know how deeply you care for me. I have not been in a position to ask, and I dare not ask you now. I found out only today that it is necessary for me to continue this trip alone. It may prove dangerous. Please help me to keep to this decision."

"No, John, no! You cannot go on treating me this way. You know how much I care!"

"Darling, it is not as I had hoped, but destiny has such turnings. We must accept the situation and pray to God our separation is only temporary."

Mary's eyes filled with tears. She looked tenderly and pleadingly at John. She had been so sure he would not leave her again. But he had made the decision, so there was nothing left for her to say.

They spent the last precious moments together. It was hard to plan a meeting place when neither of them knew anything about where they were going. John said if they lost contact with each other Mary was to try to find him through the Mormon Church in Salt Lake City. He promised to get word back to her at Council Bluffs, if possible.

They stood hand in hand, voiceless and tearless as they approached the dock at St. Louis. For the others there was great joy and excitement. The other members of Mary's family had assembled all their luggage in a pile and were ready to leave the boat.

When at last the boat was made fast and the passengers were able to disembark, John said to Mary, "Come, I will help you with your baggage."

The Thomases all waited on the pier for the time when the boat would go on and John would have to leave them. Mr. Thomas knew there had been a romance between his daughter and John but had not considered it serious. Now he saw how pale and sad Mary looked, and knew otherwise.

Outwardly John appeared calm and reserved, but underneath he felt sick. Even if he had decided to ignore the dangers and ask Mary to go on with him, he was sure her father would have forbidden it. Fate had decreed that they should part, he told himself, but surely they would meet again.

Mary put her hand to her throat when she heard the boat whistle to signal its imminent departure. She looked at John, their glances held a moment, then he turned to bid her family good-bye. Little Hannah began to cry. Mr. Thomas and Sally wished him well. "Take care of Mary," he said, and then put out his hand to Tom.

"Au revoir, old man. Don't forget our night at the helm. I pray your life will never get that rough again."

"I don't expect it to, but you can never tell."

John, taking Mary by the hand, moved a little apart from the others. "Please, don't look so sad, Mary. Have a little confidence in me. I am counting on seeing you again."

The boat whistled its last warning. Before he rushed away he whispered, "Sweetheart, keep praying for us."

"Oh, John, I have prayed!" she said, and he left her standing there.

Mary could not bear to see him go so she shut her eyes, forcing out the tears that were hiding there. On the boat John stood looking back and clutching the rail until his knuckles turned white. Leaving Mary was one of the hardest things he had ever had to do. But as the boat pulled away, he felt proud of himself for having been strong enough to do it. Once more he felt like the man he used to be.

CHAPTER NINE

It seemed to John the farther up the river they got, the more antagonistic the people were. In certain localities just to claim membership to the Mormons was to invite trouble.

Having no one but himself to protect now, he was in no mood to tamely take insults from anyone. The missionaries, after listening to some of the things John had heard, looked seriously at each other, and one said gravely, "If I may presume to advise you, Brother John, keep away from those men as much as you can. They mean trouble."

At the next stop one of the missionaries returned to the boat with a large bundle and handed it to John, "Here, put these on," he said. "I think if you change your attire, those hecklers will leave you alone. They seem to have singled you out because they can tell by your attire you are a foreigner."

It made a miraculous change in John's appearance. With a hat and boots he looked a foot taller. The next time he strolled down the deck the troublemakers stepped aside without noticing who he was.

When John and the other Mormons debarked they were immediately besieged by horse traders, wagon makers, guides, and suppliers of every item needed to outfit the emigrants for their travel west.

John purchased two fine horses and an elaborate saddle. It took nearly all his money, but he figured that in Salt Lake Territory they would be worth as much or more than what he paid for them. Farther west, he had been told, they used the system of barter and trade more than money.

By the time John completed his purchases, and found the camp where he met his friends again, they had already started to get the wagons loaded and lined up for departure. It would be a long and perilous trip and no one wanted to get started late in the season because of the scarcity of both food and water for the stock while crossing the sunbaked prairies.

John had his pack about ready and was admiring his new outfit when a large, burly fellow with black whiskers rode up at such a gait that when he pulled his horse up, it threw sand and dust all over the road and John.

"Traveling with the Mormons?" he asked.

"Yes, sir."
"Any family?"
"No, sir."
"I'm Brannan, Bill Brannan, master of that wagon train over there going to Salt Lake Territory. This your outfit?"
"Yes, sir."
"Could get along with one horse, couldn't ya?" He didn't wait for John to answer.

"Scouts just returnin' report a scarcity of feed through the prairie country. Fires and more wagon trains 'n usual gone through. Gotta cut down on everything with a belly, else I'm afraid they'll go hungry along the way."

"I couldn't take all my stuff on one horse, sir."

"I can see that, but what you gonna do with damn stuff like that," he said, pointing to a fancy carved box that contained a few little trinkets of Dorothy's. "That kind of stuff is strewn all along the way. All you need is powder and lead, food, and matches. You Mormons don't need room even to tote a bottle of licker or a chaw of tobaccer."

"But, sir, I . . ." John started to argue.

"Don't 'sir' me, Englishman. The name's Bill. Just plain Bill. You can do as you damn please about the extra horses; there's no law agin' it. But I plan to shoot him if we run out of feed."

He rode off as abruptly as he had come.

John reluctantly decided that Bill Brannan was right and started sorting out his belongings. He was forced to leave behind many things he treasured.

As soon as he had finished repacking, he mounted the horse he had named Buck and led the other one back to the trader from whom he had bought it.

The first part of the trip, from the Mississippi River to Council Bluffs, was made with little difficulty compared to some Brannan had made. John was anxious to get to Council Bluffs because of Mary. He expected the Thomases to arrive there ahead of him.

The day the guide announced they would be in Council Bluffs before nightfall, John dusted his clothes, shined his boots, and dressed with great care. He told the wagonmaster he had business in Council Bluffs and wanted to be released from helping set up camp. He would meet them at the river site.

"That's all right, Griffiths," Brannan answered. "You have done more than your share already."

As they neared the settlement, John thought of many things. He was lighthearted in anticipation that tomorrow he would take himself a wife.

In spite of the great cloud of dust the wagon train made, many people lined the road. When Brannan halted the column opposite the United States barracks John left the caravan. He rode along slowly searching in vain for the face he longed to see. Word had gone out in town that the wagon train just arriving was made up of Mormons. Scouts had carried the news ahead. John was sure Mary would be among those standing along the road. When she wasn't there he rode down the main street into town. Traveling by boat, the Thomases should have been there long before him.

John inquired at all the stores and blacksmith shops for Daniel Thomas. He had begun to lose hope when at one place a bystander heard John inquire after a blacksmith who might have recently set up a shop there and said: "There's a man out a ways that does some horseshoeing in his barn, but I don't know his name. He's a foreigner of some kind."

"Thanks, that sounds like the party I'm looking for."

It was getting late, but John was so sure he was on the right track that he rode five miles out into the country only to find it was not Thomas.

It was after dark before he got back to the Mormon camp. He was worn out from disappointment and a long, hard day in the saddle. There were still a few sitting around the campfires, but John was not in the mood for talking. He unrolled his blankets under a supply wagon and was soon asleep.

The next morning he arose early in order to leave camp before anyone was up. He wanted to leave before Brannan could assign some task and continue his search for Mary. He still had hopes of finding her.

He very nearly combed the town without finding a trace of the Thomases. Passing a school, he suddenly thought that if they lived near town, Hannah might be in school. The schoolmaster tried to be helpful.

"And have you been to the docks, Mr. Griffiths?"

"The docks—of course! How stupid of me not to think of that."

"I would inquire there for people coming up the river. If

your friends have come, there would be a record of any cartage they freighted in."

John wasted no time in getting to the docks. But officials there had no Thomases on their records. John learned, however, that no boats or barges had been able to make it up the river since the flood began and none were likely to arrive as long as the water kept rising. Because of the heavy snowfall that winter the high water might not subside for some time. John was extremely worried when he heard that several boats attempting to make the trip had been swamped and some of the passengers drowned. There was nothing he could do but wait.

The wagon train was also halted by the high water. But after several days Brannan began to get restless. These delays were costing him money, and he would have to return during the winter if they didn't get started soon. He had crossed the river once before in high water, though not this high, and realized the peril. But on the day the water receded a few inches he called the travelers together and told them to get their belongings in order, because as soon as the river had dropped one foot, he planned to move the vehicles across. This didn't take long.

There were some, including John, who didn't want to try crossing yet. "It doesn't look safe to me," John said.

"Ah—come on, John. We all know you are stalling to give that Thomas girl more time," Brannan said, and the others laughed.

John didn't say any more. He wasn't afraid for himself, and if the men with families didn't protest, he would let it drop. In any case, they all knew it was useless to oppose the wagon master.

The crossing was made without any serious mishap. Here they had the aid and equipment of the people of the town. The Platte River, however, would have to be forded without help. This worried Brannan, but he hoped by the time they reached it the high water would have subsided.

They followed the Platte as closely as they could without trying to cross it. There were days of drenching rain when they had to drag the wagons through the mud, and at night there was no dry place on which to camp. Then it would turn hot and soon clouds of dust from the alkali desert, driven by fierce winds, would burn their flesh and blind them.

The days dragged into weeks, but they kept plodding along. As yet they had not encountered any hostile Indians, although word was spread that they were now traveling in unfriendly territory, and Brannan advised everyone to be on the lookout. One never knew when there would be an attack. They did know the Indians had been there as the prairie had been recently burned for several miles along the route. John was glad now he had not insisted on bringing the extra horse. He spent hours of his time separating the charred clumps of prairie grass so Buck could get the inside unburnt portion to eat.

When they got into buffalo country, scouts were sent out in search of the herds. Hunters were chosen, not only for their ability with the rifle but for the speed and endurance of the horses they rode. John was one.

On one of these buffalo hunts they had their first encounter with Indians. They had been riding for several hours, following the base of a low ridge of hills, when one of the men in the lead shouted back to the others, "I haven't seen any fresh sign all morning. How about riding over this ridge? I don't think we'll find any buffalo here."

They all turned their mounts and headed for the top. As soon as they could see over, they stopped the horses in their tracks. Below them a vast prairie spread out into the distance. Less than half a mile away was the largest herd of buffalo they had seen. Two dozen or more Indians were ready to make a kill.

The Indians immediately saw the men, and one of the redskins gave a yell. All the others formed a circle around him. Evidently he was the leader.

The men from the wagon train were about to turn and run, as they were outnumbered two to one, when suddenly the Indians rode madly toward the buffalo, yelling and shouting and waving their arms to stampede the herd.

It was a sight John long remembered. They hurried back to the wagons without any meat, arriving not long after the noon meal. Bill Brannan was much conerned over the incident and gave orders to get the wagons rolling as soon as possible. He instructed the drivers not to halt as long as the animals could keep going.

"Those Indians'll wanna get revenge for havin' their huntin' party upset," he said.

They had now crossed nearly three hundred miles of desert. They had suffered through several days of withering heat during which a hot wind cracked their lips and burned their skins. Their clothes were soaked with perspiration. The animals were beginning to feel the lack of water, especially since so much of the grass had burned. They had scarcely anything green to eat.

A glad shout went up when Brannan announced they would come to water by nightfall. On that day, John was riding far in the lead. After a while he decided to walk for a change. His horse, Buck, was trained to come when he whistled, so he fastened the reins loosely so the animal could graze.

Several times John noticed Buck looking ahead with his nostrils distended as though inhaling freshness in the air. Finally the horse quickened his pace. He would not come back at John's whistle.

John had never seen him act like that before. He hardly knew what to do. At first he thought there might be Indians with other horses skulking along just over the ridge. He wondered if he should start back to the wagons to warn them of possible danger, but he did not want to lose his horse and everything he owned that was tied to the saddle. Therefore, he ran after Buck whistling and shouting for him to stop. But the horse only ran faster and was soon out of sight.

John rounded a knoll and saw his horse standing over a waterhole, water dripping from his nostrils. A crudely whittled weather-bleached sign stuck in the sand beside the water cautioned: "POISON."

CHAPTER TEN

John ran to Buck, hoping against hope that he had only cooled his dry and cracked nostrils by dunking them in the waterhole. But as he came closer, he could see by the girth of the saddle that the horse had drunk his fill. Looking about him, John could see scattered on the sand the whitened bones of other animals who, like Buck, had let their thirst overcome their instinct for self-preservation.

John knew there was no way to save his horse. He took a powderhorn from the saddle and swung it over his shoulder while he removed his bedroll. He had already taken his gun from the saddle before he let the horse run loose. A man never walked in this territory without his gun. He cursed as he tugged on the cinch for slack to loosen the saddle from Buck's already swollen belly. He did it roughly and angrily, thinking only of himself and the predicament he was in without a horse. But then Buck rubbed his nose against him, and John felt a tightness in his throat. Buck was his nearest and dearest possession, and now he was going to have to kill him. He berated himself aloud for letting the horse have free rein in the face of so many dangers. Buck stood for a while with his head low, looking dejected, as though he knew he should have come when John whistled. He seemed to be awaiting his fate. Presently his eyes grew wild and bulging. He reared upon his hind legs and squealed and pranced about, frightened by the intense pain inside.

John saw a shadow cross the sand and looked up to see buzzards circling in the air above the waterhole, somehow knowing that a meal was coming. John knew that as soon as the animal was lying helpless they would descend and start tearing at his flesh, even before death had come. He quickly reached for his rifle. He wanted to shoot the scavengers and scare them—but he knew what he had to do.

His hands trembled. Although it would be an act of mercy, it was not easy for him to shoot his horse. Just as he started to fire, Buck turned and looked at him as though he understood what was about to happen and the shot went wild. The horse started to run. John quickly reloaded the gun. He was afraid the horse would get away and suffer needless agony. But before John had time to pull the trigger a shot rang out from behind him and Buck fell dead in his tracks.

John turned to see Bill Brannan lowering his rifle. "Thank you, Bill," he said. He was relieved that Buck had not gotten away to die a slow and agonizing death out on the prairie.

"It ain't a steady hand a man has when he aims at his horse," Brannan said. "I hurried to do it for ya. I feel it's partly my fault for not warnin' ya, but ya weren't nowheres to be seen when I give warnin' ta the others about this waterin' hole. After this, I shouldn't have to warn ya to stay closer to the wagons. My God, man, what if the Indians had moved that sign away? You might have met the same fate as your horse. Now, get your saddle and climb on behind me. We've gotta get back ta the others."

The next morning John arose long before the others, took up the saddle, and began to walk toward the west. As he passed the lead wagon, old man Sutton peered out from under the canvas top to see who was stirring so early. When he saw it was John he said, "Good mornin', lad. You're startin' early, eh?"

"Yes, I have to or I won't catch up with the wagons before dark. You will pass me soon enough," John answered walking on.

"Sorry I can't help you out, but I can't haul another ounce. You know I took on the Davis family when their team played out back in the burnt grass country. Davis and I have had to walk much of the time ourselves so that the children and womenfolk can ride."

John knew Mr. Sutton was right. Nearly everyone with wagons was hauling the goods and the families of the less fortunate who had either lost their outfits crossing the flooded rivers or whose horses or oxen had played out along the way. It was not uncommon to see a woman crying over a treasured possession which had to be tossed out to make room for another man's family.

As they traveled on west each day the dark blue range on the horizon commenced taking shape, and they could see they were approaching the Rocky Mountains. Often during the day John stopped to rest. He could feel the metal on the saddle burn through his shirt. He tried to get a little sleep during the middle of the day, but it was too hot and seldom was there any shade. Hope still guided him as it did all the Mormons, and no matter what hardships they met, they explained it as "the will of the Lord." They did not complain over any task they had to perform.

In spite of his early start, John could see that the wagons were forging ahead of him. By dark he was trudging a mile behind.

The stillness of the night was broken now and then by the howl of a coyote. There was no sound more lonely than a coyote's as it echoed out across the prairies. John was not a coward, but he gave a sigh of relief when he approached camp and heard the sentinel call out, "Who goes there?"

"John Griffiths, a two-legged beast of burden," John replied.

Someone called out, "Get him some oats." John took the jesting good-humoredly, but was too tired to take part in the nightly service. Away from the sounds of the meeting he was soon asleep.

His plight was discussed at the service where one of the Mormon leaders announced: "John Griffiths' horse died so he is walking and carrying the saddle. I expect some of you to make room for his load and give him a ride too, now and then."

There were some who had not heard of John's plight since he had not asked for help.

Scarcely a day passed as they neared the fort that they did not meet one or more bands of Indians, mostly squaws and children, going to or from the fort and trading post. The Indians moved noiselessly and would stand at a distance, watching. One thing that amazed the travelers was that the animals belonging to the Indians were as quiet as the Indians themselves. John hoped they would meet some with horses to sell, but Brannan advised them not to bargain with the Indians or encourage them to loiter around the camp, or the next goods they bought might be their own.

It was a happy group of people that circled into Fort Bridger, and none was more happy than John to be relieved of his saddle. He soon struck up a favorable trade with Jim Bridger. He was not so easily taken as when he first came to this country. However, Bridger was not the typical horse trader. He was known all over the West for his honesty, not only in his dealings with white men but Indians as well. John traded the saddle for a horse, some provisions, and a small amount of gold. Good Mexican saddles, silver trimmed like John's, were scarce in this territory.

The Mormons did not spend much time at Fort Bridger. They were eager to get on to Salt Lake City. Leaving the fort they traveled all day, constantly descending. The trail was lined with quaking asp and in places went through box canyons where overhanging rock nearly shut out the sunlight. Finally they emerged into a beautiful valley with plenty of water and grass. It was a temptation to stay there, as it was the kind of place that those intending to settle were looking for. It was hard to get the cattle headed away from the good pasture, but they continued on, crossing Bear River, then Yellow Creek.

The western side of the Rockies was more difficult. They now entered a country of deep canyons of straw-colored rock and queer-shaped pinnacles formed by weather and time. The road ran along perpendicular cliffs, sometimes a thousand feet above the valley floor. Some of the women were afraid to ride lest the wagons slide over the narrow ledge and go hurtling down. They were often delayed by fallen rocks in the road, so large it took five or six men to move them before the wagons could get past.

They were changing their course southward now, through the beautiful Wasatch Range; through upland valleys and canyons where pines and aspen scented the air. One day after they had entered an especially high boxed-in canyon, Bill Brannan called a halt and told them this was their last descent. This canyon would bring them out into the Great Basin of the Rockies which only three years before had been ceded by Mexico to the United States. The Mormons knew about that, and knew it had been a great disappointment to their leader, Brigham Young. He had wanted all this territory for the Saints and he still claimed it. It was known to them as the Provisional State of Deseret, not the United States.

Once again the train stretched out and wound on down the gorge following a stream that ran the full length of it. The wagons crossed and recrossed it, constantly descending until they came directly out of the canyon and turned west down the draw. There was a slight rise ahead; when they reached it Brannan pulled the lead wagons to a halt, forming a semicircle so that everyone could see ahead.

It was a bright clear day and as the wagons approached, the people were awed by the magnificent sight below. The desert was spread out in all its glory, with the Great Salt Lake shimmering in the distance. The weary emigrants shouted with joy at the sight of it. Smoke from the city brought forth another burst of rejoicing. They had been so long away from civilization and its luxuries they could hardly wait to get there.

They could readily understand why Brigham Young, arriving at this same spot four years before, had declared, "This is the place!"

The weary missionaries, returning home from abroad, were glad to have arrived. But this territory was new to them also as they had gone to Europe from Illinois. These men, John Griffiths, and several other Saints who were riding ahead were met by a welcoming committee that had come out to meet the wagon train.

After receiving a cordial greeting, they rode on to the churchyard. Here a band was playing, and the women were preparing a feast for them. They were received with hearty hospitality.

Now several other men hurried forward to greet the missionaries. John recognized Brigham Young as being the man he and his mother had heard conducting a meeting in Liverpool. Young had made such a deep impression on John then that he had not forgotten him or his voice. Now, after all these years, he was being introduced to the famous leader.

When Brigham extended his hand, John hesitated. He did not want to do the wrong thing. Here in America customs were different. But when he felt the firm clasp of the leader, he sensed the true meaning of freedom. Here he was shaking hands as an equal with one of the great men in the nation. He didn't have to cringe before him. His spirit burned with exaltation, and as the band played patriotic airs he zealously pledged his life to this great country. He felt as if he had touched something he had spent his life searching for.

CHAPTER ELEVEN

Salt Lake City was the only large settlement between the Missouri River and Sacramento, and since the gold rush it had flourished because so many travelers passed through it on their way to California. Although the big lake was found to be seven times saltier than the ocean, there was plenty of good water from other sources. The Jordan River and City Creek flowed through the center of the settlement.

During the winter and early spring, following the arrival of the first Mormons, the group planted 5,000 acres of grain to insure food for the large companies of colonists expected to come. With a group like this John felt he could not help but succeed.

A few days after the new settlers arrived a special meeting of the city council was called. They were to be advised how and where to obtain free land, and any questions they might have would be answered by the council.

When John arrived at the meeting he noticed that the men who made up the city council were the same ones who had made up the church committee that met the wagon train on the day of their arrival. The business of the city and that of the church seemed to be one and the same.

Those just arriving were told that tools and supplies would be issued from the great warehouse of the church and could be paid for later when the crops were harvested. This was good news to those with little or no money. There was so much being offered to them it was overwhelming. John remarked that he was beginning to understand the meaning of democracy. When he spoke of it, one of the committeemen replied, "Out here we can't travel each man for himself. We have to divide, no matter how slender our stores, and if you get sick or downcast we won't desert you. Feel free to call on us anytime."

The settlers who arrived late in the season would not be able to plant any crops until the following spring. For these people, Young had several projects going. Much of the region west of the city was covered with water, from a few inches to a foot deep, from the lake. A drainage system had been started. By building dikes and ditches the Mormons were reclaiming hundreds of acres. Also they were building a sandstone and adobe wall fifteen feet high and three feet thick around what was called the Temple Square as a make-work project for the unemployed.

When John was not helping on one of the projects, he gave his time to the church. Because of his friendship with the missionaries since before he left Wales, he was treated as one of them and soon became closely associated with the heads of the church. Eventually he was asked to serve on the advisory board. John found in Young's employ both good men and those he felt were not the sort who should belong to the church. He wondered about this but decided that a few undesirables were bound to creep into such a large organization.

Whenever John had time he looked for land. He could hardly make up his mind which direction to go. The mountains were beautiful and majestic, but one could not raise wheat on a snowcapped peak. Most of the valley was a barren, salt-encrusted desert, and the ground was worthless without water. John was awed by the bigness of the country. One could look across the desert and know that even when it faded from sight it went on and on. The mountains behind the city rose abruptly seven thousand feet above the valley floor. There were no gently rolling hills to connect the two.

It made a man feel he would be swallowed up by the vastness of it if he tried to conquer this land. Only two sorts of men had tried it—brute men who professed no faith or fear and men like Brigham Young who had such deep faith in Almighty God that they possessed an inward strength nothing could break. John could not help admiring and respecting this courageous leader—one who had tried and won.

When the fall harvest started pouring into the markets and the church warehouse from the outlying districts, a great abundance came from the farms in the Provo River Valley, some fifty miles south of Salt Lake. John was anxious to see this region where wheat produced thirty bushels to the acre. The following spring, with his friends Ben Evans, Bill Parrish, and Parrish's two sons, Mr. Lewes, and a man they called Tom, he started out to explore that part of the country.

After they had ridden hard for a time they stopped on a knoll and scanned the country in all directions. The sun, just coming up over the Wasatch Range, cast a glow over the desert. Looking back toward the Great Salt Lake they saw the sun's reflection on the water, and what looked like glistening white sand around it. They knew this was salt and thought it a shame that so beautiful a valley could be so worthless.

"Aren't we ever going to get away from that damned salt?" asked Ben Evans.

Profanity was seldom used by the Mormons. No one answered Ben. A good Mormon ignored the salt. Brigham Young stressed that his people should not complain.

John broke the silence by saying, "I wonder what it is like at the head of the Jordan River?"

"I thought you knew. Utah Lake is the source of it," answered Parrish.

"I've heard of that lake. Isn't it a small one?"

"Yes, compared to Salt Lake. It is over twenty miles long, however, and seven miles wide, and it is fresh water."

John wondered about that, but didn't want to ask.

They rode on and did not stop again until lunchtime. They had passed the marshes by then, and the land along the river was beginning to show green, with patches of aspen here and there not yet leafed out.

The men sized up each piece of ground they looked at. Nothing had excited much interest among them so far, the region being mostly sagebrush and sand. Sometimes they would draw rein and look a little longer at a piece of ground, then silently ride on, each with his own thoughts and evaluations. Several times they rode off their course to inspect a green patch on the mountain side of the road, but none of them wanted to be that far away from a settlement because of the danger of Indian attack.

The church advised the people to group together rather than scattering. The Mormons were friendly with the Indians, and the chief, known by the name of Walker, had recently become a member of the church. But there were bad Indians as well as bad whites. The chiefs themselves were unable to put an end to raiding parties.

It was dark by the time the men came to Dry Creek. Both they and their horses were tired, so they agreed that this was a good place to spend the night.

Early the next morning they were on their way again. Utah Lake came into view first, and then they could look into the valley where the Provo River ran into the lake. The valley was small but the greenest they had seen. It was surrounded by high mountains covered with brush and trees, the taller peaks capped with snow. The river was larger than they had expected, and the lake was surrounded by a lush growth of reeds and swamp grass.

even the sagebrush was larger than usual.

"It is a beautiful valley," said John. "I know how Brigham must have felt when he first saw Salt Lake Valley and said 'This is the spot!' I have the same feeling here!"

"Me too," said one of the others. "Let's go."

Because of the marsh the road swung far to the left before crossing the river. At Provo a group of people had gathered at the roadside to greet them. The men had watered their mounts at the river, so they stopped only long enough to satisfy the curiosity of the settlers. Then they went on to Springville, some seven miles farther.

It was the same at Springville. The people had seen them coming and were waiting. By now John had made up his mind he wanted land here if he could get it. The abundance of fresh water, the richness of the soil, the proximity to timber, and the prevalence of wild game were some of the things that made the area attractive to him. Springville was so named because of its large spring of clear water, with an outflow sufficient to run a mill.

Settlers had arrived there less than two years before. It was situated halfway between the mountains and the lake. Hobble Creek, lined with cottonwood trees, ran through the center of the settlement. A man named Steward operated a store inside a small fort. John had a letter of introduction from the Salt Lake Church to a Mr. Perry, president of the Springville ward.

After dismounting, the men shook hands all around and answered queries from the people.

John then asked, "Could one of you direct us to Brother Perry's home?"

A man answered, "Yes, but Brother Perry is not at home. Could I help you? I am Aaron Johnston, bishop of the church."

John replied, "I wish to see about getting land here, and so do some of my companions. We were told that we had to draw for it."

"That is right. All the good farmland has been surveyed and plotted so that everyone may have a fair share. The number of each plot has been written on a piece of paper, then put in a box from which the drawings are made. The maximum amount each man may have for irrigation is twenty acres. All who draw may have but one piece bordering the lake. Andrew Steward has charge of the drawings, and his place is right over there."

"Thanks. That is all we need to know."

John and Bill Parrish each drew for land. John said he would rather have his land out some distance and have more of it, because he thought the Thomases might come out when Mary did. So he drew twice and got Lot 1 in Block 11, bordering on the lake, and 30 acres more removed. Both men were pleased with what they drew. Their land was a short distance back toward Salt Lake. They started out at once to look at it.

John was proud to be a landowner, even though it was thirty acres of brush and ten acres of tall reeds and swamp grass. He envisioned what he could make of it.

He moved to Springville as soon as he could wind up his affairs in Salt Lake City and began immediately to get his place in order. He worked as long as there was daylight, then lighted a lantern and continued into the night. All his life he had hoped to own land, and now that he had it he enjoyed the labor.

Neighbors told John he couldn't get ready to plant crops that season. Nevertheless, he did. Then he went to his ten acres and started clearing a place for a house. He worked hard all week, but did not fail to ride to the settlement each Sabbath to attend church. He missed his friends in Salt Lake City and sometimes would go in and remain several weeks, helping with the erection of the church buildings in exchange for supplies and seed from the warehouse.

On February 23, 1853, just before John moved to Springville, ground was broken for the Mormon Temple. There was an all-day celebration. It was a great day for the Mormons, and they all pledged work and donations. At that time John pledged so much he had to neglect his own place to keep it. The temple was to be built of solid stone, so that it would last until the millennium. Its six great spires would be seen from all over the valley. For Brigham Young the erection of the temple would be the fulfillment of his fondest dream. The Mormons had been forced out of the eastern part of the United States because of their way of worship. The laying of the cornerstone represented their freedom. Now they had their own state in which to live and worship according to their own plan. And although there was not an inscription to say it, they saw the temple as a symbol of the "blood and guts" it had taken to conquer this vast desert. Neither cold nor burning heat, hunger nor disease, not even the great lake of salt had deterred these crusaders. Now the temple would be a shrine to their convictions.

Whenever John went into Salt Lake City he inquired at the church for a letter or other message that might be there for him. He did not give up hope that Mary would come, yet he was not sure the Thomases had ever arrived in Council Bluffs. Mr. Thomas might have decided to stay in St. Louis or to settle in some other region. John was not sure Mary had received his letter asking her to come. But he never doubted her love and her intention to wait for him. Because he was betrothed to her, he shunned all social gatherings not connected with the church and kept busy working on his land.

But when spring began to blossom, it struck John that his life seemed empty. In July there was a break in the work while he waited for the crops to ripen. He walked along the lake, deep in thought, the silence broken only by the plaintive call of the turtle doves. It reminded him that his plans for the future were not working out. He felt a deep loneliness when he saw the doves flying away in pairs.

"I am going into the city and seek some friends," John said aloud.

He knew several young women in Salt Lake City, any one of whom would make a pleasant companion if he could only forget Mary. He resolved to shut the door on another unhappy chapter in his life and try to find a wife.

CHAPTER TWELVE

When Mary Thomas heard her father and brother coming home from work, she took the iron teakettle from the stove and left it on the bench outside the door so they could have hot water to wash off the grime.

Mr. Thomas washed first as he always did. Then he went inside. Mary came out to get the kettle, and her brother, who was combing his hair in front of the broken piece of mirror, beckoned to her urgently.

"Close the door. I have something to tell you."

Mary closed the door, then playfully cupped a hand behind her ear.

"Don't let on that I told you," cautioned Tom, "but Pa has a letter that some strangers left at the blacksmith shop this afternoon."

"For me?"

"He didn't say. But the men were from the Salt Lake country."

Mary gasped, and her face grew flushed.

"Maybe it's from John."

"Your guess is as good as mine," Tom replied.

The two went into the house for supper.

The others were seated already at the table. Mary helped the children fill their plates and while doing so upset Benny's milk. Her father noticed her nervousness and guessed that Tom had told her about the letter. He wished Tom had not done so, although he was glad there was this close relationship between them.

Mary took food on her plate but was too nervous to eat it. If the letter belonged to her, why did her father keep it? Why did he not say he had received it? Whenever she glanced at him, he was looking steadily at her. He appeared to be weighing some decision in his mind. She could not keep her hands from trembling.

Supper was over, and still no mention was made of the letter. Mary and Letticia did the dishes, and little Hannah unfolded the tablecloth and put it back on the table. Mr. Thomas and Sally worked outside, spading a garden patch. Tom milked the cow. Even Benny had a chore—throwing the table scraps to the chickens. He was still so small that sometimes the dog or one of the cats would jump up and knock the dish from his hands, and he would run crying to the house.

Finally the day was ended and the whole family was assembled in the one room that served as kitchen, dining, and living room. They were awaiting the nightly Bible lesson. Mr. Thomas also read the mail, if any, at this time. It had been the custom to read all letters aloud so that everyone could enjoy them, because so few letters were received.

Sally took down the Bible from the shelf. Her husband wiped his glasses on the red-checked tablecloth, turned up the wick of the kerosene lamp, then took the Bible. But instead of opening it he laid it on his knees and drew the letter from his pocket.

Sally sprang up, saying joyfully, "Oh, a letter!"

Mr. Thomas turned the letter over in his hands several times as if debating whether to open it. Finally he said to Mary, "Daughter, this is for you."

Though she had yearned many months for this letter, she almost wished it had never come. It was *her* letter. How could her father read it? "Please, Father, may I have my letter and go up now to my room?"

"Not until the reading of the Scriptures is over," he replied.

He placed the letter on the table and began to read aloud from the Bible. Mary felt like snatching the letter and running out of the room, but she was afraid to do it. Never in her life had she defied her father. So she sat back in her chair though she heard scarcely a word he read.

After what seemed ages to Mary, he laid the Bible down and said, "Good-night, children. You may go to bed."

All of them except the baby slept in the attic where curtains served as partitions between the beds. Tom and Letticia went upstairs first. Sally busied herself dusting off the Bible with her apron, at the same time taking a closer look at the letter. Little Hannah loitered around the bottom of the stairway, not wanting to go up to bed. Always before when there was a letter she was allowed to stay up and hear it read. Even three-year-old Benny sensed something was in the air. He sat on the floor picking kernels from several ears of corn that had been kept behind the stove to dry for seed.

Mary did not know what to do. Was she to go to bed like the others while her father opened her letter, or was she to take it with her? Upstairs there was only a candle and she shared part of the attic with Hannah and Letticia.

At last her father moved away from the table, leaving the letter there. Sally started to turn the lamp down, but Mr. Thomas said, "No, let the lamp burn so that Mary can read her letter."

Mary went to the table and sat down in the chair where her father had been seated. She just sat there, looking at the envelope, hoping Sally and her father would go on to bed and allow her to read it by herself. It soon became apparent they had no intention of doing this, so she opened the letter with trembling hands. There was no alternative but to read it before them.

"Why, this letter is a year old," Mary said in surprise. She looked first at the signature. It was from John, and read:

Salt Lake Territory
1852

My dear Mary:
 After a hard and perilous journey we arrived in Salt Lake City. I find it to my liking. I have established myself with the church. Mr. Young is a great and soul-inspiring man. I have a one-room house now. I am sorely in need of a housekeeper. I have prayed often that we will meet again and hope this will reach you. Since you were not in Council Bluffs when we went through I have been worried about you. We had quite a time getting across the river there.
 If God be willing and with your father's consent, I beg of you to be my wife. I have waited long to say these words and hope you do not disappoint me. Enclosed is a letter asking your father's permission for you to come. If your answer is what I think it is, please deliver it to him.
 Maybe your family wishes to move on west. There is good land here for the taking. There are great possibilities here. I hear more settlers are to come from Wales. Maybe you could travel with them; they are more gentle in their manners. It would be nice if Tom could come too.
 With deep affection and may God bless you and your family.

 With all my love,

 John Griffiths

Mary sat for many minutes, rereading her letter over and over. It was so good to know that John was still alive and cared for her. There was not a doubt in her mind what she would do, even if it were against her father's wishes. She would run away if it became necessary.

Mary decided not to deliver the letter John had written to her father until the next day. She wanted to keep it a secret, at least until she had told Tom. She placed both of the letters back in the envelope and started for the stairs.

But her father arose and extended his hand. "Daughter, may I read your letter now?" he asked.

She had no choice but to hand him the letters.

Sally stood reading over her husband's shoulder. Mary was not angry with her, for she knew the arrival of a letter was an exciting event for her hardworking stepmother.

Mr. Thomas slowly removed his glasses and sat in thought for a few moments. Tears came into his eyes. He loved Mary dearly; he did not want to lose her. At last he returned the letter, saying, "Mary, God bless you, my daughter, and help you make the right decision."

After John had made up his mind to go to town he lost no time getting ready. It was nearly fifty miles to Salt Lake City. The weather was extremely hot for July, so he left before daylight, clad only in breeches, boots, and hat. His good clothes were neatly folded and wrapped so they would be protected from the dust, then hung over the packsaddle of his other horse.

John was happy as he set out. While he would much rather have been going to meet Mary, it was good to have come to a decision on an issue that had been bothering him for a long time. Working his place alone, often doing the work a woman could be doing, was holding him back.

As John rode along he thought of first one female acquaintance and then another, considering the kind of wife each would make. He found that none captured his fancy. But, he mused, there were lots of girls and women in Salt Lake City that he did not know, and he would have to mix more socially and get acquainted with some new ones.

Before reaching the city he stopped at the river, washed up, and put on his good clothing. In all his years of farming he was never slovenly about his dress.

John was in fine spirits when he went calling on his old acquaintances. He began to accept all the invitations he received. He was surprised to find that many of the Welsh girls he had known on the way out to Salt Lake—any one of whom he had thought would accept a proposal from him—were already married. It caused him to wonder if Mary also had tired of waiting.

One night while he was riding around town to kill time he heard music. He went to investigate and found there was a dance at one of the wards. John edged his way through the crowd of young men outside the door. Inside, he leaned against the wall beside some other spectators and looked the crowd over. The music roused his senses, and he suddenly wished he knew how to dance. He wondered now why he had never before thought about dancing.

A pretty girl danced by, hanging over her partner's shoulder. She did not miss John's roving eye. Between dances she sauntered by, and he saw that she was not as young as he had thought. She stopped short in front of John.

"You ain't dancing, huh?" she asked.

"I'm not a dancing man," John answered.

"Then I shouldn't have saved this one for ya', huh?" she said, leaning closer.

"I guess I'd better say good-night, miss," John said, and hurried outside.

"Whew," he said, as he got on his horse, "I didn't intend to work that fast."

After he had stayed in Salt Lake a few days, wandering around and doing nothing, he grew tired of being idle. He went to the temple site and started to work. He owed quite a few days of work to cover the pledge he had made the day the cornerstone was laid. He enjoyed working more than wife-hunting. Every time he started hinting to a woman that he had matrimony in mind, she became so willing that he shied off.

A group of settlers arrived and John was asked to ride out with the committee to meet them. He searched every wagon for a familiar face. One man told him a blacksmith and his son in Council Bluffs had repaired a wheel on his wagon. They fit the description of Mr. Thomas and Tom. John was deeply hurt. Now he knew for sure that the Thomases had settled in Council Bluffs, and he decided that Mary must have received his letter and failed to answer deliberately.

John was so despondent he felt in need of counsel and prayer, so he called on John Smith, patriarch of the church. The minister suggested that he bestow a blessing on John which would give him courage and more power in the House of the Lord. John knelt before the patriarch while the special prayer was said:

This twenty-fourth day of July, 1853—Brother John, in the name of Jesus Christ I place my hand upon your head and seal upon you the blessing of a father because you have come into the order of the priesthood for your own salvation and that of your father's house. The Lord is pleased with the integrity of your heart, and he has appointed you to lead your father's house, to bring them into the new and everlasting covenant, that they might be saved back to where they died in the new gospel, to the dispensation of the fullness of time, that they might be gathered with the righteous in the last days. You shall have a companion to assist you. Shall be able to multiply your posterity according to the desire of your heart. Your posterity shall be numerous as the sand upon the seashore and be great in the priesthood and mighty saviors upon Mount Zion. You are to preach the gospel to many people. You shall have power to speak the language of any among whom your lot is cast,...shall be satisfied with the fruits of the earth, shall see your Redeemer stand upon the earth, shall live and reign with Him a thousand years and unhurl all the blessings of His Kingdom with all your father's house.

Amen.*

Now that John was in the priesthood it was hinted that he should take himself a number of wives in order to carry out the patriarch's prophecy that his posterity be "numerous as the sands upon the seashore."

Although polygamy had been denied publicly until a few months before, it had frequently been discussed among the church members, and the practice was admitted before John by some of the elders and Brigham Young himself. The reasons for it were supposedly spiritual. On one occasion when John was seeking more information about it, he was instructed to study more deeply certain chapters of the Bible as well as his Book of Mormon. When he entered a higher order of the church he would be able to understand the revelation and see that the Mormons were following the ways of Jesus Christ, the Father, and the Holy Ghost, he was told. John let it rest there, although he was not satisfied with the answers.

The blessing bestowed upon John by the patriarch gave him new hope, and he hurried home to wait a little longer for Mary.

The crops were ready to harvest. John had stayed away longer than he had planned; now everything needed to be done at once, so he threw himself into his work. He finished his house in the way he wanted it. He built a boat and enlarged his platform at the lake, where he spent more time than in the house. He no longer lifted his eyes from his work to search the road to see if anyone was coming. He'd decided he couldn't spend his life watching and yearning.

One day he worked from sunrise until late afternoon in the big field farthest from the lake. The harvest was stacked in two piles, one for himself and one for the church. He was very pleased,

---
* *Recorded in Book G, page 506, No. 1238, Salt Lake City*

since the grain had run more than thirty bushels to the acre. The whole field was now under irrigation. Now he could afford to buy more cattle and have plenty of feed to get them through the winter. He was pleasantly occupied with his thoughts and did not see two figures approaching on the high road coming from the north. The road from Provo to Springville went along the foot of the mountains. As there were no settlements between, it was plainly visible from either of John's places, but from the road to the house at the lake it was nearly a mile.

As soon as John got back to the ten acres where his buildings were he put the horses in the shed, fed them, and started to the house to get some food. It was not until he was on his way to the house that he noticed the riders coming. They had already turned off the main road onto the lane leading into John's place.

He hurried into the house, washed up, and combed his hair. It was uncomfortably hot and he knew that whoever they were, they and their horses would be thirsty. When he went to draw fresh water from the well he saw that one rider was a woman. He walked leisurely toward them, not letting himself hope it was Mary. As they came nearer he waved his hat and then, all at once, he could see that it *was* Mary—and Tom! He could hear Mary laughing as they raced their horses toward him.

CHAPTER THIRTEEN

Tom sprang from his horse and ran to shake hands with John. "Well, at last we're here!" he exclaimed. But Mary hung back, suddenly shy. It had been over two years since they had parted, and John looked so different. She had never seen him in western clothes; she remembered him as he had looked when he came from the old country.

Tom, seeing the fresh water dripping from the bucket, ran to get a drink.

John went to Mary and held out his arms to help her down.

"How I have prayed you would come," he said. He had meant only to help her from her horse, but when he held her in his arms and felt her breath against his throat, he kissed her lips, her eyes, her hair. Again he realized how lonely he had been, living with only the memories of their being together on the boat.

Mary responded to his embrace, shedding tears of joy. Finally John said, "Would you like to see our house?"

"Mind if I come along?" Tom asked. He had returned from the corral where he had put the horses away. For the moment they had completely forgotten him.

They entered the adobe cabin—one long room with a sod-covered roof. John had started it as a two-room house but after he gave up hope of Mary coming he had never partitioned it. There was a huge fireplace at one end, built for cooking as well as heating.

"You have worked so hard...you have done so much," she kept repeating.

"There is still much to be done. I have only started, but it will be easier now that you are here. Why did you not come last year?"

"I did not receive your letter until this spring—it was a whole year old. I came as soon as I could after I got it. Letticia came too. She is working for some people in the city."

"If you left this spring you were a long time on the road. Did you have trouble?"

"Oh, we have been in Salt Lake a long time. I left word at the church, then waited for you to come. I have something important to tell you!"

"What is it?" John asked curiously.

"While we were waiting in Salt Lake City there wasn't much else to do so Letticia and I went to church, and after a few meetings decided to be baptized in your faith."

"I am glad," John said, "but I still don't know why you didn't come sooner."

"Then we heard you had been in town and gone. I wondered why, so went to the church and asked about my letter and found they had not given it to you."

"Why didn't you come on to Springville after you found out where I was?" John asked.

"We were advised not to make the trip by ourselves, so we waited until some others were coming to Provo and we came that far with them. I was undecided whether I should come at all."

"Yeah, she was afraid you might already have two or three wives," Tom teased.

"Oh, you silly thing, I was not," Mary said.

"You were too; I heard you and Letticia talking nights, making plans for when you got to Salt Lake City. It made Mary awfully mad when Letticia said if it was true that the Mormon men had more than one wife maybe she could marry up with you, too."

"Well, I did think of getting me a few wives. Those young women that came across on the boat with us are still here and as far as I know some of them are not married yet." Then, in a more serious mood, he said, "I am sorry to admit it but the church is having some trouble over polygamy. But I think it will be ironed out. The Mormons are very righteous people, and Brigham Young hasn't revealed all the particulars about it yet."

Outside he showed them the boundaries of the place and how far he had ditched the water from Hobble Creek. He pointed across the valley to where he had the other thirty acres. John never tired of showing his place. It was an obsession with him. No one born in free America could understand his feeling about owning land.

Mary expressed delight over everything that he showed her. She went several times to the well remarking about the cool water. She spoke of the advantages of having water from Hobble Creek for irrigation, but never once did she go to or mention the lake which was the outstanding feature of the place.

John was very proud of the lake. He had spent hours of hard labor cutting through patches of reeds and huge bunches of swamp grass higher than his head to open up a way to the shore.

He had taken great pains building a walk and ramp out to the clear water where he tied his boat. He had used the peeled poles intended for partitions in the house to build it. When he had the time in the evenings it was a pleasant place to sit and think.

John noticed Mary's lack of enthusiasm over the lake and guessed what was passing through her mind but decided not to tell her right away that she was mistaken. Before dark she walked slowly—as if she were going against her will—to the end of the ramp. Dipping some of the water up with her hand, she placed her tongue into it, tasting. "Oh, it isn't salt at all!" she exclaimed.

John had followed her. "For shame, Mary," he said. "All this time you have held an indictment against the Lord because you were so sure the water was salty like the Great Salt Lake that you wouldn't even mention its beauty."

"But, John, who are we to be so lucky? This is a blessing from heaven! Isn't it wonderful! There is nothing else we need hope for."

"Well, yes, there is a little thing like a marriage ceremony that hasn't taken place yet."

"I know that as well as you, my lord and master."

"You left some things in Salt Lake, didn't you?"

"Yes, I wasn't sure we would be staying."

"Mary," he said, and gently kissed her, "are you now?"

"Yes, John. I was sure I loved you but wasn't sure if you had changed your mind."

"As long as there is a trip to be made into Salt Lake City, let's go tomorrow. I would rather be married there. I wish the Temple was ready to be used, but we can be married in the church. Out here we are still having services in the fort."

Early the next morning all three started out for the city. John took an extra horse and packsaddle to bring their luggage back. It took an entire day of hard riding to make it. They stayed overnight with the people Mary and Tom and Letticia had traveled out with in the wagon train, and with whom Letticia was living. They were overjoyed to see Mary and Tom so soon and to meet John. The next morning plans for the wedding were made.

On September 11, 1853, John Griffiths and Mary Thomas were married in the Mormon Church in Salt Lake City, in the state of Deseret, later known as Utah. It was a simple wedding, with only Letticia and Mary's brother Tom present and the elders of the church for witnesses. But it was solemnized by all the ceremonial garments and sacred vows of the Mormon Church. They were filled with reverence and awe as they were united husband and wife.

John and Mary started in at once, working harmoniously together. The nearest neighbor was nearly a mile away, but they did not mind, as that was the way life was for settlers. Mary gleaned in the fields, and did the housework and cooking as well. She also found time to weave material, to sew, and to knit. In the old country she had learned to weave and braid straw, so she even made the hats that they wore at work in the fields. She also made baskets from willow shoots, in which she carried the eggs to market. It seemed to John there was nothing she could not do.

The little mare that John had bought in Salt Lake City just after their marriage was gentle as a kitten and became a regular pet. One day Tom said, "You know, that little mare you bought will climb a bank or walk anywhere. I saw her walk out on that ramp a while ago. She is just like a nanny goat."

John had forgotten to ask what her name was, but from then on they called her Nanny. Mary claimed her for her own horse.

The shed John had built the year before for a barn could not hold that year's crop. It was Tom's job to go to the mountains and chop down trees for timbers for a new and larger building. He could go to Hobble Creek Canyon and follow the left-hand road to the top of the mountain where the timber started or he could go straight across from their place to the big mountain and zigzag up and around a steep and dangerous precipice until he finally got to the top. One way took about as long as the other. It looked as if there had been a big landslide some years before, which left a place on the edge of the mountain almost perpendicular.

One day Tom noticed the faint sign of a trail. It appeared that at one time this path had followed around the overhanging face of the cliff, but it had kept caving in until in some places the whole ledge was gone. No doubt it had been used by the Indians to shorten their distance to the valley, but no one had ever been known to ride a horse around it, although the Indians often rode their ponies over places that seemed impossible to the white man.

Tom kept thinking how much time it would save if he could only use that old trail again. One day he worked his way around to where a mass of loose sand and rock had slid down the canyon a hundred feet or more below. It didn't look so dangerous, and he decided with a little work he could make the old cutoff usable. That would save a lot of time getting to and from the timber.

He went to work, digging it out a little more on each trip he made. A short distance around it he would hit a good road on top of the mountain. He worked with a shovel and sometimes with his ax, and in a place or two where it was solid rock and he couldn't use either he spanned the gap with poles. At last he decided it safe enough to try his horse.

Then Tom received a lesson in horse sense. The animal would only go where Tom had dug the trail out along the bank, but refused to take another step forward. He could see he was at the brink of a cliff. Tom tried every way he knew to make him go on but he wouldn't be led. Tom had to give up.

He didn't tell Mary or John about his trail building, but the next morning he asked Mary if he could use Nanny to ride to work. Mary said he could, supposing that his own horse had a loose shoe or something.

Tom rode Nanny up to where his own horse had turned back. She, too, sensed the danger. She could see below and knew what her fate would be should she make a false step. It was a foolish and dangerous thing for Tom to attempt. But when he got off and started leading her, Nanny went right along. In a place or two her sides scraped the side of the precipice, but Tom coaxed her on. A few times around and Tom had no trouble riding her, though he had to pull his legs up going past the places where she scraped the side.

When he came back so quickly, dragging poles, John was astonished. He cautioned Tom about running Nanny, so Tom told him about the trail and how he had saved miles on the trip going up.

John went with Tom one day, and after seeing the trail he refused even to walk on it.

"It isn't safe," he told his brother-in-law. "The formation of that cliff is soft sand. You can see up there where it keeps caving in a little all the time. The whole thing is apt to sheer off any minute."

John also told Mary not to let Tom use Nanny, so he couldn't ride around it. No one mentioned the trail again.

It was a pleasant year for John and Mary. She made him feel his importance, and he reveled in the fact that Mary looked up to him for the man that he was. She honored and respected him for his strength and leadership. She was proud of him for his refusal to endure suppression, while Dorothy had been made miserable by his rebellious nature.

When John could get away for a while they made a trip to Salt Lake City in order that he could work some more on the Temple. Mary accompanied him because she was anxious to visit Letticia. Some time earlier she had received word of her sister's marriage to John's friend, Henry Moore. Now that she and Letticia were both married, they would have lots to talk about.

Tom went with them to Salt Lake City and remained there when John and Mary returned to Springville. He had been offered a man's job with a man's pay and he did not like to turn it down. Besides knowing the blacksmith trade of his father, he was a mechanical mastermind; even as young as he was, he had gained recognition as a skilled workman and eventually became something of an authority on the erection of sawmills. He was much sought after to choose a site for a mill and to assemble it.

CHAPTER FOURTEEN

When John and Mary left Tom in Salt Lake City he said he would not be home until spring, so Mary was surprised to see him riding up only three days later. When she saw his pale face she knew he brought bad news.

Tom took hold of her arm and led her into the house and sat her down on the bed. "I have a letter from Father," Tom said gravely. "Mary, little Hannah is dead."

"Oh, no!" Mary cried.

"Pa said she went after the cows and milked them, brought the milk to the house, and all of a sudden took violently ill. They sent for the doctor, and he came right away and said she had cholera. The doctor stayed all night, but early in the morning of August 27, Hannah died." Tom's voice broke, and he could say no more.

John came to the house as soon as he saw Tom's horse there.

"What's my partner doing back?" he asked lightly. But then he saw Mary lying across the bed crying and Tom sitting beside her, grave faced.

"What is it, Tom?"

"Our little sister died," Tom answered.

"Little Hannah!" John said. "How?" Tom told him the sad story.

Both men knew Mary would blame herself and rue the day she had left Hannah to come west to marry John. Sure enough, she said sadly, "Poor little thing, she was doing my work. It is my fault for leaving her."

"No, Mary, no more than mine," Tom said.

John tried to comfort them, but there seemed to be nothing he could do or say that would alleviate their grief.

After Mary gained control of herself she said, "Please tell me what else he had to say, Tom."

Tom drew the letter from his pocket and scanned the pages. "He says they have been doing very well. He earned four hundred dollars this spring, and they have plenty of hay and grain and gold and silver. He bought a house and lot and tools from a wagon master for sixty dollars, then sold them for one hundred and fifty. They have moved into town. They had everything loaded on the wagons ready to come west when high water came and they were afraid to cross the Missouri River. He said people had been forced to camp there on the banks of the river for nearly four weeks before they could get across."

"I know what that river is like. We had the same trouble, and then lost several outfits getting across," John said.

"We found out how treacherous it was, too," Tom added. "We saw an old lady fall off the boat and drown when we were coming to Council Bluffs. The captain wouldn't let any one try to rescue her. The river was boiling, and he said if people got into it they could never get out. We waited in St. Louis so long for the water to go down I thought we would never get out, and Mary was having fits all the while lest you would leave Council Bluffs before she got there."

Tom continued reading the letter. "He got ready to leave again and he got a felon on his finger, and then it was too late in the year to start. Now they intend to come in the spring. He wants you to find him a job, Mary, and to write before spring and tell him all the things he should know about the trip. There is a postscript at the bottom that says he loaned five dollars to John Reese, thinking he would follow with the next bunch of people going through. He says if you can collect it you can have it."

"Poor old Reese," Tom said, laughing. "He doesn't have a chance once Mary gets on his track. He will have to pay or be hounded to death." He passed the letter to John.

"He closes by saying to give his love to all the Saints. That's funny for him to say, when he isn't one of us," John remarked.

"I wonder, does he mean the polygamists, too—or maybe he doesn't know about them yet," Tom said in a tone of disrespect.

No one answered. Mary was feeling so sad over Hannah's death she did not hear him. John did not approve of Tom's mocking the Mormons. He was, at present, a dedicated member.

John and Mary believed that Joseph Smith and Brigham Young were prophets as surely as they believed in Jesus Christ. They tried hard to accept polygamy as a revelation from God. Some of the members went so far as to say they did not believe it was a revelation at all—that Young had made it up because it was something he wanted to do. But John did not believe that.

Obedience to the leader of the Mormon Church was considered a supreme duty, and John knew he was disobeying counsel by having only one wife. He knew his rise in the church would be cut short if he made known the fact that he never intended to have more than one wife. John hoped and prayed polygamy would die from its own corruptness. He had Dorothy and Mary sealed to him in a ceremony of celestial marriage. He hoped that would satisfy the elders for a while.

"Oh, I almost forgot—I've got more bad news," Tom said. "It seems that the Indians known as the Tintics, living around the southwest shore of the lake, are causing trouble." The Indians hardly cared what the Mormons did in and around the Great Salt Lake, but now these pioneers were taking their good land and pushing them away from the clear water lakes, out into the desert. John's place was just on the other end of the lake from the Tintics.

The settlers could usually tell when the Indians were enraged about something. They would start by stealing horses, killing cattle, and sometimes sending raiding parties out into the settlements. They would kill as well as plunder. A killing happened at Spanish Fork, south of Springville. A few days later a rattlesnake skin wrapped around a bunch of arrows was found hanging on another settler's door. This served as a warning and declaration of war.

"I heard that Mayor Wood called a special meeting at which a decision was made to build a strong wall around the fort," Tom said.

"They have been talking about that for some time. Now maybe they will," John said.

"Out of logs?" Tom asked.

"No.... a mud wall—something like the one in the city," John answered.

"I'm staying here until these Tintics settle down. It seems to be a general uprising, for old Chief Walker of the Utes is mad, too. Said the Mormons broke their treaty with him and got over into his domain," Tom said.

Although war was declared by the Indians, it did not prevent Brigham Young's coming to Springville to carry on a series of meetings. He warned his people not to allow even the local Indians into their homes, however, and he advised the women and children to stay at the fort until the uprising was over.

John's thirty acres were closer to Springville than the rest of his property; however, he chose to put his buildings on the ten acres bordering the lake, twice the distance away and considered just outside the border of safety. Young personally cautioned John and advised him to bring Mary to the fort.

Some Indians passed around the lake and through John's place almost every day, and he had befriended many of them in one way or another. He believed, therefore, that they would remain his friends. He feared the marauding bands of Indians that had no particular tribe and roamed about in search of plunder. They were always around if there was a war.

After a few days at the fort, Mary returned home. Either John or Tom stayed near at all times, and they were never without their rifles, even in the fields. John tried to get Mary to go back to the fort but she wouldn't.

The winter passed without any serious incidents with the Indians. In the spring, peace was declared, and things settled down.

As soon as the ground was dry enough to plow John got the big field ready first and sowed it all to grain. He and Mary had already figured out on paper what they expected to make out of this year's crop. From the grain and increase in stock, they figured they would be able to get nearly everything they wanted.

"I'm going to see about buying some more stock with my share," John said, then asked, "Tom, what do you plan to do with yours?"

"Oh, I don't know...hadn't thought about it. I don't have much use for anything more than a good horse and gun and I already have them. I'll help you and Mary until Pa gets here."

"On the contrary, you must take your share. You have worked as hard as I have," John insisted. "We will split three ways as we agreed."

"I don't believe in counting chickens before they're hatched, but if you did get so much money for your grain you'd have trouble spending it, I might see about getting a lot or two in Springville or Provo for a blacksmith shop, now that Pa is coming," Tom said.

"That's a good idea, but you know I drew for two plots of ground—one of which was to be your father's."

"I know that, but he would never take it. He would want a place nearer town or at least on the main road where he could have a shop. Blacksmithing is all he knows."

"It's up to him," John said.

"I know several things I am going to buy, but it is still a secret," Mary said.

After a few weeks of warm spring weather John returned to the back field to view his planting. Where a plowed field had been, soft blades of grain covered the ground, making it a verdant green. It always gave him pleasure to note the changes that occurred in his crops from one day to the next.

Then came the afternoon John returned from the back field and said, "These hot days have sure dried out the ground. That big field is just baked; we will have to irrigate it tomorrow. If we start early and all hands at it we should finish before the heat of the day. I'll ride over and see if I can get that young Indian, John Pants, to help us."

There was a story behind that name. Mary was always helping the Indians in one way or another but disliked having them stand around half naked. One day she gave this particular young man a pair of John's trousers, told him to put them on, and not to come again without them. He never did. This so amused Tom that whenever he saw the Indian coming he would say, "Here comes John's Pants." Soon he was known everywhere by that name and even called himself John Pants—pleased to have a white man's name.

"Glad you mentioned the irrigating, John, or I would have been gone before sunup. I found out where I can get some iron. I want to put iron around the wheels of Mary's buggy. Did you notice how fast the wooden wheels wear down in this sand?"

Tom had found an abandoned buggy, brought it home, and repaired it over the winter so Mary could use it to transport the butter, eggs, and bread to the store to be traded for other things.

"I will help tomorrow, too, John, but as soon as Tom gets my buggy finished I want to go to Springville and show it off. I am so happy over it, Tom. I am sure I will have the nicest buggy in the whole valley," Mary said.

"You had better see how Nanny likes it first. She might not respond to being hitched up as well as you think she will. You might have butter and eggs scattered from hell to breakfast," Tom told her laughingly.

"That little gentle darling, she wouldn't run away," Mary said confidently. She loved her horse.

"You can never tell. I've seen them go plumb loco having something they can't get away from dragging behind them," John said.

"Don't worry, John, I will try out Nanny first," Tom promised.

Even before the sun came up, the water from Hobble Creek was gurgling in the ditches and the thirsty ground drinking it up. They kept repeating over and over how tall the grain was and how full the heads, exuberant over what promised to be a fine crop.

"This patch will run over thirty bushels to the acre, don't you think?" John asked.

"Yes, I do. It is a bumper crop."

They ate a midmorning lunch that Mary had brought along, then rested awhile, waiting for the field to get a good soaking.

"I noticed a few grasshoppers...see, there's one. They kept falling into the ditch," Mary said.

"Well, I hope they stay in the ditch. I've heard if they get thick enough they can just about take a crop," John commented. "Mary, you go to the lower end of the field and start shutting the irrigation gates down there, and work your way toward home. Tom and I will go to either side and work up toward the main gate. The ground seems to be wet enough. I think we can finish in an hour."

"I hope so. It's getting awfully hot," she said.

"Here, John Pants, I'll pay you off. Thanks for helping us out," John said to the Indian boy. He handed him a silver half dollar which was generous pay. Farm labor was forty cents per day and keep.

As John walked along, he noticed that the grasshoppers were steadily becoming more numerous. They actually appeared to be coming out of the moist earth. They were everywhere. John saw the grain falling to the ground under their weight. They were devouring the crop!

CHAPTER FIFTEEN

"Tom, get on the horse and go to the barn and get sacks...and hurry! The grasshoppers are taking the wheat!" John yelled.

There weren't many grasshoppers on Tom's side of the field yet, but he did not stop to ask questions. He could tell by John's voice it was urgent.

With the sacks they tried to shoo the insects away and mash them into the ground. They weren't making any progress with the sacks so John tried covering them with dirt, but they came right up through it and swarmed over the grain.

John and Tom could see Mary at the other end of the field, waving her apron and pounding the ground with it, so they knew the grasshoppers were getting into the field from all sides.

"I think they are coming out of the ground, John. We can't do anything with them."

They wet the sacks in the water and began beating the grasshoppers to death, trying to save their crop. They worked desperately for hours, and killed great piles of them, but they could see it was all in vain. They knew that before the grasshoppers were gone the crop would be completely destroyed.

John and Tom labored side by side, as they had at the helm to save the ship at sea. Their bodies were dripping with perspiration, their eyes red, and their lips swollen. They lay down on their bellies and drank the warm water from the ditch to dampen their parched throats, pushing back the bugs with their hands. The sun beating down on them was well over a hundred degrees.

"We can't do any more, Tom. It's no use. We haven't stopped them, and we have already lost the best portion of our crop. There will not be enough feed for the stock this winter—and barely enough for ourselves. Again I have failed." John sat in the soggy field and held his head in his hands.

"You can't blame yourself for an act of God," said Tom.

"I guess not. It does not appear to be his holy will for me to succeed here on earth."

Tom did not know what to say to John in the face of this disaster so he went to the house, exhausted and disappointed—not for himself but for John and Mary.

John sat there awhile, benumbed by the disaster. All at once he thought of Mary. He had forgotten all about her.

He stood up and began searching the field, his hand shading his eyes. He could not see her anywhere. He ran to the spot where he had last seen her and began calling, but she did not answer. Always on the alert for Indians, he became alarmed and ran through the field calling frantically, "Mary! Mary! Where are you?"

The soaked ground was hard to walk on. Finally he came to her tracks. He followed them and found her where she had fallen from the heat and fatigue. The next moment he sank down beside her. He gently wiped the hair and dirt from her forehead with his hand, wet with water from the ditch. Her face had been burned by the sun. John blamed himself for asking her to work in the field. Mary finally opened her eyes and smiled faintly.

"Darling, why did you keep going until you were overcome? I never want you to work this hard again."

"It was not the work, John. I am with child," she told him.

"Oh, Mary, why did you not tell me this before? I would not have allowed you to be working out here today."

"The baby will not be here until winter. Are you glad about it?"

"I *am* glad. It is wonderful that our good Lord has rewarded us. Now I must make the house warmer and hew out some fine boards for a cradle, and never again will I let you work in the fields."

John helped Mary to her feet and they walked slowly down the road to the house. "We must tighten our heartstrings to endure this loss that undeniably was the will of God. Why, we do not know. His ways are hard to understand at times. It is a strange thing that he allows our food to be destroyed and at the same time gives us another mouth to feed."

John was deeply moved over the news that he was to become a father, yet he wondered why good things always came to him accompanied by disaster. He realized they might be facing a famine, as the crops of others in the valley must also have been destroyed.

All of the wheat was gone except patches here and there where a few bunches were left. These ripened lying on the ground. Mary went out with a bucket and picked the grain up with her fingers, trying to glean enough for their own needs for the winter.

It was a backbreaking job, day after day in the burning heat. John tried to persuade her not to do it in her condition; he said he would turn the hogs in on it. That way it wouldn't be a complete loss, because as soon as they were fattened up he could butcher them for winter.

But Mary refused to let one grain of it be wasted. Every day she would salvage close to a sack of wheat, and she seemed almost as happy over this as she had been over the whole field, because it was something she had saved from nothing. It also meant they would have flour for winter and a little left over to roast to take the place of coffee. If she was very careful there would be a handful now and then for Nanny.

When John saw he could not stop her, he and Tom joined in, and though it was a slow process John was really surprised when he saw the bin in the barn was full and quite a big stack of it sacked up besides. Without Mary they would not have bothered to salvage any of it. She not only saved the wheat but dried fruit and vegetables for the winter. Whenever she added something more to the larder she liked to show the men.

"John, have you heard how everyone is talking about a famine this winter?" Tom asked.

"I've heard some of the farmers were hit as hard as we were, but the church will see to it that everyone has enough food, I think."

"It's not the winter I am worried about. I'm afraid we will starve before it gets here, the way Mary is hoarding all the food we have!" Tom was proud of his sister, even though he teased her constantly.

"Do you know it will soon be winter? Did you notice there was snow on the mountain? And before spring there will be another mouth to feed," John said. "Help me to put this together will you, Tom?"

John was making a cradle and fitting the sideboards into the ends.

"It's awful little. It doesn't look big enough for Flossie's kittens," Tom said.

John did not want Mary to be alone at this time so he got a young Indian woman who did housework for various families to come and stay. They were not sure when the baby would arrive but knew it would be soon. There was no doctor available, but they had a neighbor who was a midwife. She would come as soon as Mary needed her. She delivered most of the babies in the community, so they weren't worried over not having a doctor. Mary was only disappointed that Sally was not there to care for her when she had her first child.

On December 10, 1854, between eleven o'clock and midnight, a son was born to John and Mary. Mary wanted to name him after John, and John wanted to name him after his brother Henry, so the baby was called John Henry Griffiths.

By spring Mary was working in the fields again. Watching her coming toward him, John marveled at her strength. She carried the baby astride her hip and a load across her shoulder, yet her small body moved gracefully across the field. John could be a completely happy man now if it were not for the trouble in the church.

Polygamy was becoming the subject of much controversy. It was breaking up families. There was actual fighting at the church meetings. Brigham Young knew something had to be done.

All the Saints were summoned into the city to attend a meeting at which time the leader was to make another speech on plural marriage. It had been nearly two years since he and Orson Pratt had first proclaimed polygamy as the will of God. Those like John, who were not sure it was God's plan, hoped he would denounce it. Those who followed in the footsteps of their leader and now had many wives and children hoped he would not, as it would be embarrassing to have polygamy proclaimed adultery.

At the meeting Brigham not only openly sanctioned it but defied the power of the United States Government to stop it. Many left the church and went to California. Others, including John, stayed on, still uncertain, or with so much at stake they could not afford to move out.

Church leaders started testing the loyalty of members. They were after John again to take another wife, but he was a man who did not like to be dictated to and he certainly would not enter into something against his own desire. Mary was bitterly opposed to it, and when John reported what he had been advised to do she sprang up from her chair and exclaimed fervently, "I will foreswear my religion before I will allow another woman to live in this house!"

There was now a nonpolygamist group forming in the Midwest.

Even before polygamy was declared Mormon doctrine they claimed they were the true followers of Joseph Smith. John was not one of them, but he kept trying to oust the evil from his church. He had no success because the worst offenders were those highest in the church. Brigham himself now had twenty wives. All the heat and anger that had been built up against polygamy in secret was now out in the open. There were killings on both sides. John began to fear for his own life and even more for Tom's. He cautioned Tom again and again not to make sarcastic remarks about polygamy, but Tom was young and hotheaded and ready to fight.

The battle was not being fought openly or fairly. Men were stabbed in the dark or found shot in the back by arrows, making it look as if Indians were the culprits. Those fighting against polygamy were being removed from their positions in the church. John began attending less frequently, still hoping that in time polygamy would die of its own corruptness and the fighting would stop.

One afternoon in the late fall Mary put Johnny into his cradle, covered him snugly, and went to the window to draw the curtain when she noticed movement in the distance. She watched only long enough to see it was not the wind blowing up dust, but a procession of some kind coming toward their place.

Her first thought was Indians. She rushed to the cradle, snatched up the baby, and then ran toward the barn calling for John. He came out immediately. The baby was screaming at the top of his voice, having been awakened so abruptly, and John thought something dreadful had happened to him.

"What is it, Mary, what happened to him?" John asked, trying to take the baby from her arms.

"No, John, not the baby...Indians!" she cried, pointing toward the road.

John could see the dust rising. "It's a bunch of them. Let's get out of here fast."

Tom climbed up on the fence to get a better view.

"Don't look like Indians to me. Looks like a bunch of cattle, some horses without riders, and two prairie schooners."

By now they were nearer, and John thought he knew who they were. He turned to Mary, who was trying to quiet the baby.

"Here, let me take him. I think you will be tearing down the road in a minute. It's your father."

Just then Tom shouted, "It's Pa!" and started running toward them, with Mary at his heels. But all at once she thought of her sister, little Hannah, and could not go on. She turned and walked back to stand beside John when the Thomases drove in.

Her heart could not contain the sadness she felt, and she broke down and cried in her father's arms. He, too, wiped tears from his eyes. Tom felt sad, but showed no outward emotion. John brought Mary the baby, and this helped her regain her composure. There was another outfit with the Thomases; Letticia had come from Salt Lake City to show them the way.

Now that Mary wouldn't have to be alone, John and Tom journeyed into Salt Lake City with two loads of grain, one to be ground into flour and the other one to add to the church warehouse supply to help those less fortunate. They camped overnight on the way. When they arrived in the city at the crossing, where they would go in different directions with their loads, John shouted back at Tom, "I'll have the wheat ground, then meet you at the Moores."

When Tom arrived at the warehouse there was already a farm wagon backed into the unloading platform, so he pulled alongside and waited. A girl was sitting in the other wagon. Tom waited for her to look up. When she finally did, he smiled and started to speak. Tom was gregarious and liked having someone to talk to, but she turned her head quickly away as if she were spurning conversation. Tom saw enough of her face to decide she was the most attractive girl he had ever seen.

He was starting to get out of the wagon when an old man came to the door and yelled at her in a stern voice, "All right." That was all he said, but the girl understood.

She climbed down quickly from the seat into the back of the wagon and started to drag one of the sacks of grain into the warehouse. It was so heavy she staggered under the weight of it.

Tom sprang forward and picked it up to carry it for her, but she ran along beside him, saying, "Please, please, mister, put it down. I will carry it myself."

"You carry this?" Tom laughed, looking at her size.

"I can drag it, so please, put it down. Jake will see, and he'll be awful mad that you spoke to me."

"Jake be damned," Tom said. "It's too heavy for you." But Tom noticed she was trembling and in tears so he put it down, just as the old man appeared. He spoke angrily to her for not having several sacks unloaded.

Tom sat in his wagon and watched her for a moment. Her eyes were big and beautiful, but there was no radiance in them. Her lips were red and full, but without a trace of a smile. Her whole expression was one of despair. Tom wondered what she would look like if she smiled. It was hard for him to sit there and watch while she dragged the sacks out of the wagon, but the old man she called Jake stood guard. After she was gone Tom could not stop thinking of her. He had never before been interested in any one girl. He loved his horse and his gun, and he had a good home with Mary and John.

When he met John he told him how the old man had made the girl unload the grain.

"And you permitted it?" John asked.

"I was unable to prevent it," he said.

On the way home Tom made up his mind to return to Salt Lake City in the near future and find out who those people were. He also decided to get hold of some land of his own. If he ever did want to settle down, he had nothing to offer a woman. Tom had never thought along these lines before.

CHAPTER SIXTEEN

There were rugged old shade trees to which farmers hitched their wagons around the store that Henry Kern operated in the front of his house in Springville. The church had been completed, and the store had been moved out of the fort, which now housed the school. Although the settlement was still small, it was beginning to look less like an outpost.

Mr. Thomas decided to settle in Springville. That pleased Mary, and John offered to help him build an adobe house.

Tom kept wanting to get back to Salt Lake City. He could not forget the girl he had seen at the warehouse. However, it was several months before he was able to get away. He and John had their work to do on the ranch, and he helped his father get settled.

From the start Mr. Thomas was busy. He wanted Tom to stay and help, but Tom said he had promised the millwright where he had worked that he would come back and help him for a week or two. Even John did not suspect the real reason Tom was going to the city.

On arrival Tom went to the Moores and delivered a letter to Letticia from Mary, then sauntered down the street. He noticed a crowd gathering at a church meeting and he went in. The girl he was looking for wasn't there.

"It isn't going to be easy to find her in a place as big as this, when I don't even know her name," Tom mumbled.

He returned to Moores and went to bed. Riding from Springville, he had been a long time in the saddle.

The next day, Sunday, Tom rode past the church again, and spotted a team and wagon that looked familiar. He tied his horse and went in. The room was quite full, so he stood in the back and looked for the girl he had seen unloading the grain. He soon found her. She was looking toward him, and he could tell by her expression that she recognized him.

Tom smiled and started toward her, but she quickly turned her head and put her hands up to shield her face as though she were afraid her looks might betray her feelings. Tom stepped back and stood at the rear of the church with a group of young men, thinking he would seek her out as soon as the meeting was over. Then he noticed that the man the girl had called "Jake" that day at the warehouse was sitting in the same row with her. There were several older women seated between them.

Tom whispered to the young man standing beside him, "Could you tell me the name of that girl sitting on the bench to the left of us?" He nodded his head in her direction.

The fellow followed Tom's gaze, then whispered back, "She's no girl; she is one of old man Jessup's wives. That's him on the other end of the seat, and all those women sitting between them are his wives too."

This news made Tom sick with disgust. It roused in him both pity and hate. It was plain to see the girl was not happy. Tom was disappointed, but the feeling now ran deeper than that. He felt as if he had been robbed of something. How was a young man to find himself a wife when all the girls were being sealed in marriage to these old men? These polygamists were getting bolder every day.

As the meeting got under way the members became more and more emotional. Tom was about to leave, then decided to stay a while longer and watch what went on. He sat down near the back.

Most of the congregation did not participate in the "sealing of wives" ceremony. The ones that did went to the altar, singing and praying and clapping their hands. Tom kept watching the girl. He had made up his mind that if she gave any indication she wanted his help he would give it to her, but when she got up and joined the orgy along with Jake and his other wives, it was more than Tom could stand. He was so riled that he forgot John's warning, and rose up and shouted: "Why don't you call it stealing wives instead of sealing wives?"

Someone in the crowd said "Amen," and several who heard Tom's comment began to laugh. The elder who was performing the rites was furious over the outburst and laughing. He said, "Will the party causing the confusion in the back either get out or keep quiet?" Everyone looked to the back of the room.

Tom was already starting to leave. He turned at the door and said, "I was leaving of my own accord. I despise an organization that lures innocent young women astray." He stalked out.

Outside he mounted his horse and rode quickly away without looking back. Nevertheless he was aware that three men had come from a back door and had run toward their horses.

Tom knew the men had not left the meeting for the same reason he had; suddenly he remembered John's warnings against starting any disturbance with the Brighamites. He knew the men were following him, and he must ride fast to get away.

Tom did not stop at Moores but headed for the hills and brush country. He had a fast horse, and they would have to ride hard to catch him. Once he was screened by the bushes and sandhills he headed south toward Springville. He got home safely, so they either lost track—or were not after him in the first place.

On June 28, 1857, a daughter was born to Mary and John. They named her Hannah Mary, but for Mary it brought sad memories every time the name was spoken, and it was confusing to have two Marys in the same house, so they began to call the baby May.

In September 1857 a large emigrant train passed through Utah on its way to California. Some of these emigrants were from states where the Mormons had been cruelly treated. More recently Parley Pratt had been killed in Arkansas. This contingent of emigrants was treated coldly by the Mormons as they passed through Salt Lake City.

There were many wagons and over one hundred men, women, and children. When Mary and John saw the column of dust rising they knew it was the wagon train coming toward Springville.

"Let's take the day off, John, and go over to Pa's and watch the wagons go by," Mary said.

"All right. I might be able to help your father and Tom in the shop. An outfit as big as that will be sure to need work done at a blacksmith shop. And I heard they were not permitted to stop in Salt Lake City for security reasons."

"I would like to get there before they do. I am getting together all the things we can get along without to sell. I will take all these eggs and butter and vegetables and..."

"Now don't sell us short," John interrupted. "Tom and I like to eat too."

When they were ready to leave John could hardly get it all in the buggy.

"Mary, are you taking all our salt pork?" asked John. "Only yesterday you said there would not be enough to last until butchering time again."

"I know it, John, but it is a chance to make some money, and we won't have to trade this for other goods like at the warehouse."

John started looking into the packages.

"But you took all the butter," John complained.

"Oh, for pity sakes, John, there has never been a meal yet you didn't have enough to eat." Mary was getting provoked. It wasn't every day they had a chance to name their own price and get cash for what they sold.

It was a very exciting occasion. People lined the road as the wagon train approached. Many others had brought goods to sell. When the town and church officials noted how many women and children were in the party they advised the wagon master to go back and take the northwestern route to California, as the Indians to the south were considered more troublesome. But despite the warning, the wagon train went toward Cedar City.

John and Mary were still talking about what happy people these were when the shocking news came back that the entire outfit had been massacred at Mountain Meadows. Some said there were several children found alive—children not old enough to tell about the massacre. At first, it was reported to have been the work of Indians, and no one would ever have thought differently, but after a while it leaked out that some of the killers were white men dressed like Indians.

This was a horrible thing to blame on the Mormons. John refused to believe it at first, yet he knew there was a secret order in the church organized by the Brighamites to punish and reform those working against them. Its existence was denied, but everyone knew of it. When this order was first organized they were called the Danites; then they became known as the Avenging Angels. They were violent, brutal men who did not hesitate to follow Brigham Young's orders. They were led to believe they were performing a special duty and would be rewarded in the eyes of God.

There was no reason for the Indians who were hired to participate in the Mountain Meadows Massacre to keep still, so first one scrap of information and then another leaked out until it was positively known that the Mormons did have a hand in the planning, if not the actual killing.

This time it seemed they had gone too far. News was

received from the east that United States soldiers were headed for Salt Lake Territory to put a stop to such incidents, and also to put an end to polygamy, which, according to Washington, was against the law. Brigham Young maintained that the United States Government had no authority over church or government affairs in the Salt Lake Territory, and said the Mormons would fight, if necessary, to protect their rights. Obviously he would never, of his own accord, stop the practice of polygamy.

John took pride in being a Mormon, but he was equally proud of being an American. His highest hope was to become a citizen. If the time should come that he had to choose between the two, John would not hesitate to stand by the United States Government.

After many meetings, he and a group of like-minded men from the Springville church decided to ride into Salt Lake City to talk personally to the officials there, since Brigham had always encouraged the Saints to come to him for counsel.

They went in a body to the Temple in an attempt to end once and for all the polygamy issue that was tearing the church apart. But they were refused counsel and told to leave town. John informed the only man whom they were able to speak to at the church office that he, himself, was a member of the advisory board. He was told that because he lived in Springville he was no longer a member of the Salt Lake City board. John knew that was not the reason.

They were also told that Brigham had said, "Before I will abandon my wives and cast out my children as bastards I will fight the whole United States."

With heavy hearts the delegation from Springville prepared to leave the city.

CHAPTER SEVENTEEN

Before John left Salt Lake City he called to see Letticia and Henry Moore. He tied his horse to the gate and started toward the house, and before he reached the door, Letticia came running out to meet him, a frightened look on her face.

"John, is everything all right?" she asked.

"We're all fit as a fiddle. Why, what's the matter?"

"Oh, haven't you heard? Come inside; let's not be seen talking here." John followed her, beginning to feel alarmed.

As soon as she closed the door behind them, Letticia said, "The Avenging Angels, have you not heard about them?"

"Yes, I have. In fact, I know who some of them are. Have they been bothering Henry?" John asked.

"Not yet, but several of our neighbors have been told to keep away from the nonpolygamists who are trying to reorganize the church. And Tom—didn't he tell you?"

"Tell me what?" John was getting impatient. He wished Letticia would get on with what she had to say, for the men from Springville were waiting for him.

"About the trouble he got into here at church."

"No, he only said there was a lot of bickering going on in town and that it looked like the Brighamites were gaining footage. Is there something else I should know?"

"Yes, there is. I don't like to be a tattler, but for safety's sake, I think you should know. He got into no end of trouble the last time he was in town."

"What did he do, Letticia?" John thought of the many times he had cautioned Tom to be careful.

"He went to a meeting at the church, and when they came to the marriage and sealing of the wives he stood up and renounced his connection with the Brighamites. He was very rude and outspoken. Henry heard that the Avenging Angels chased him out of town, and now he is on their blacklist. The only reason he got away was because they were afraid to close in on him, since he's such a quick shot, but they are waiting for him to come back, and they're apt to take their revenge on you."

It was a grave John who returned from Salt Lake City. He could see the dispute over polygamy was not to be settled without a fight, and "to unsheath the sword was to put an end to hope."

Later John had a long talk with Tom concerning the incident with the Avenging Angels in Salt Lake City. "It is like fighting the Indians. You never know when or where they will strike next," he said.

"That's all right. If they want to play, I'll play with them."

"They are *not* playing, Tom. Remember that!"

But John did not heed his own warning. He'd come to America to get away from one-man power, and he had no intention of knuckling down to it now. He didn't handle his difference of opinion by raising a civil disturbance as Tom had in Salt Lake City, however. John was more easily provoked to anger than either Tom or Mary, but he did not show it. He seldom raised his voice when angered, and held his dignity if at all possible. He had learned from his father and from his own past experiences that a single word could sometimes hit harder than a blow. He was not afraid to fight if necessary, however.

Looking back it seemed to John that whenever he had engaged in a fistfight it had caused him as much trouble as his opponent. People who were close to him soon learned he was not a man of many words, but he meant what he said and would keep a bargain no matter what it cost him in the end. That was the reason he was so long in deciding to pull out of the Salt Lake City Church. Once he said he was through, he would mean it.

John and Mary regularly attended the little church in Springville, and he still held his place in the thirty-seventh quorum. In the smaller villages and outposts where there were not so many people the bonds of fellowship grew more fragile as polygamy spread. Often John left the church with a heavy heart; and Tom, since the fracas in Salt Lake City, refused to go at all. He waited for them at the blacksmith shop where he tied the horses.

Mr. Thomas rarely worked on Sunday, but there was always a group of old men sitting on a bench in the shade of a big tree overhanging the shop—the philosophy bench, he called it.

Tom noticed it was time to fetch the horses and take the carriage to the church. John and Mary were waiting out in front. John was holding Johnny's hand to keep him from getting in the dirt while dressed in his Sunday clothes. The people did not loiter after the meeting to talk as they once had, but hurried away lest they get into a heated argument with a former friend.

Even on Sunday there were chores awaiting their return. Chickens, ducks, dogs, and cats all came to meet them as they

approached, hoping feeding time was near.
"Our friends are welcoming us home," John said.

Harvest was soon in full swing so they did not attend church, though it was a flimsy excuse, for they never worked on the Sabbath. John hoped by staying at home and keeping out of arguments they would be left alone.

One morning he and Tom had just finished some chores outside and were on their way to the house when they heard the thud of horses' hooves. As they watched the approaching riders Tom recognized the big gray horse as one that had been ridden by one of the men who had followed him from the church in Salt Lake City.

He did not tell this to John, but said, "Let's hurry to the house, John. We make an awful good target standing out here." But John knew what he feared. He too had recognized at least one of the men as a known member of the Avenging Angels. That was enough to tell him this was not a social call. Tom quickly strapped on his holster. John lately was never without his.

He spoke in a low voice to Mary. "There are three men outside. We might be in danger, but don't show that we mistrust them."

There was a bold rap on the door. John wondered if they would be shot down in cold blood, or if there was some other scheme afoot. At least he would be ready for them. Tom was a fast and deadly shot, so John knew the battle—if there was to be one—would not be one-sided. It was Mary and the children he was worried about.

John walked to the other side of the room. Tom stood where he was. Both had their hands in position to go for their guns if necessary. They waited tense and ready.

Mary noticed that John's hands were steady, and that a hint of a smile touched his lips as he motioned her away from the door. She sat down on a stool close to where the children were sleeping in their homemade cradles.

"Come in," John called, clear and loud. He did not go to open the door. This made it necessary for the men outside to open the door, thus giving him and Tom a better chance. Even a fraction of a second counted in a draw.

The door latch lifted and the door was kicked open. It was

difficult for the men at the door to see inside at first, their eyes being accustomed to the glaring sun outside. This also served to put them at a disadvantage.

"Good morning, gentlemen. You are passing early. What can I do for you at this hour of the day?" John asked politely.

"We are looking for a man by the name of Thomas," one of the men said.

"That's me," Tom answered without showing a trace of fear or moving from where he stood.

"We were told you were good at picking out a millsite and that you would show us the way to the timber."

"Oh, I see," John said. "Maybe I could do it. Tom has other plans for the day." He gripped his gun tighter for he noticed Tom had dropped his hand from his holster. He didn't think Tom would be that easily fooled.

Before the men could answer, Tom said, "No, John, I'll go. I know just the place for their millsite. I was up there only a few days ago."

John did not know if he should start a gun battle here and now or let Tom ride away, to be shot down in some lonely spot or done away with in some other way and his death made to look accidental. He was sure he and Tom could win, but in doing so Mary and the children might be hurt.

Mary held back the cry that was in her throat. She knew that any show of fear might cause death for somebody. When Tom walked out the door not a voice was raised nor an arm put out to stay him. John's fingers pressed hard against the butt of his revolver, but he fell back to let Tom pass.

The men stepped backward off the porch. John followed them out, still wondering if they had succeeded in fooling Tom. If he was unaware of their trickery he would not have a chance once in the timber. If only he could warn Tom!

But Tom's next act proved to John that he had not fallen for their story. He came from the corral riding Nanny, his own prancing steed still in the stable. Nanny was used solely by Mary and they often laughed, saying the horse understood the Welsh Mary talked to her. Nanny would do almost anything Mary told her. Tom, too, had patiently taught her many tricks.

It took John but a moment to figure out Tom's plan. Then with a wave of his hand, he said, "Good luck, fellows. Hope you find a good millsite."

CHAPTER EIGHTEEN

John stepped back into the house where Mary was waiting pale with fright. She, too, figured this was some sort of scheme to make away with them. He noticed his rifle had been taken from the rack and Mary was holding it, ready to shoot. There was a look about her that made him think, There is no animal more vicious than a mother protecting her young.

"Mary, I don't have time to explain now. I must take Tom's horse and follow. I think I know his plan of escape. While I get the horses, fix a pack for Tom. He won't dare come back here for a while. Give him half of the gunpowder we have, and don't forget water. Better fill two canteens." John was rushing through the house, calling back instructions as he went through the door.

Mary measured out half the gunpowder and put it in Tom's horn. She hesitated a moment, then poured a little more. She also saw to it that there was lead and wadding in the leather pouch and a block of sulphur matches. She had everything ready and John's own canteen filled when he rode from the barn leading Tom's horse. They tied the pack and Tom's rifle on the saddle.

"I hate to leave you alone, but Tom's life is at stake. And you're right—keep that gun handy," he said as he grabbed up the gear.

"I know, John. Please hurry!"

"I dare not be far behind. I have to know which way he goes, and if his plan is what I think it is he will never get away unless I am there with a faster horse than Nanny."

Mary ran out to open the gate.

"If we are not back by tonight, take the children and go to your father's," John said as he rode away.

She stood and watched until all she could see was dust in the distance. She feared for the safety of both Tom and John, but she went to work at her daily tasks, like the pioneer woman she was.

Tom led the men through Springville and turned up Hobble Creek. He was glad his father was not in his blacksmith shop when they rode past. He might suspect and follow. That would upset Tom's plans.

The men kept behind Tom. If he slowed down so did they. They talked very little, but men riding fast very seldom do. Occasionally Tom stopped and pointed out some feature of the countryside. The men were from Salt Lake City but Tom had a feeling they had been up this road before. He could not keep from wondering if there were more of them hidden in ambush along the way. He needed time, and pondered on how to keep them from shooting him before he could use his plan of escape.

He stopped before they left Hobble Creek, pretending he wanted a drink. He hoped John would figure out his plan, and he would need time. From here on up the mountain there was thick underbrush until they reached the top and big timber. There was no one living along the way.

"We don't have to come back this way. I know of a shortcut back to the valley from the timber. It will save half the time and distance," Tom said.

"Why didn't you go that way?"

"It's awful steep, and this is the way the timber would have to come out. I thought you would want to see both sides."

Tom's answer seemed to satisfy them. The men were more interested in the shortcut, it seemed to Tom, than they were about the timber and the proposed millsite. This pleased him, because he believed he would be safe until he had showed them the shorter way out. It seemed that getting away fast meant a great deal to them.

Tom's next step was to get behind. According to his plan of escape, he had to be in the rear. But this wasn't easy. As they neared the mountaintop Tom kept slowing his horse down and working his way back behind the others. They were riding single file now. In response to a simple tug on the left rein, Nanny had been trained to rear up onto her hind legs, and with another tug she would spin around and get the horses excited. In the fracas he managed to get two men ahead of him but the third one was always behind. They were traveling slower now, and Tom kept talking about the timber so that they would not know he mistrusted them.

Once when Nanny was cutting up one of the men asked, "Why didn't you bring your own horse?"

That was a slip. If they hadn't seen Tom before, how could they know his horse? Now Tom was certain his life was in danger.

"He had a loose shoe. I was going to fix it today." Just then Nanny went into another spin.

"Damn this horse," Tom said, giving the second tug. He could make her do any trick he wanted her to do, even standing on her hind legs and rearing around. "John only keeps her to raise colts. She's hardly ever been ridden," Tom explained. Nanny went into her sidestep act and that put Tom in the rear.

"If you fellows start on she'll follow you," Tom told them.

Tom kept Nanny headed in the direction he wanted to go and waited. This was the moment. As soon as the men turned their attention to getting their horses started, Tom spurred Nanny and took off down the steep bank and out of sight onto the trail going around the precipice. It was only a short distance, but there was plenty of time for a man to be shot.

He was out of sight before the men realized what was happening. At first they thought the horse had fallen over the bank. It took a few minutes before they recovered and came after him. He could hear them calling out commands.

"Go after him, Bill!" the man who had followed him from the church in Salt Lake City called. Up to now they had been careful not to call each other by name.

Tom was waiting, gun drawn. As he expected, the man's horse would not take to the ledge. He was forced to dismount and come on foot. The others must have been not far behind because he said, after looking over the precipice, "This is a good place for a killing—accidental, of course," he added when he saw he was facing Tom's revolver.

"Accidental, hell!" Tom said. "Don't think that I don't know who you guys are. Back up fast or what happens next won't be an accident."

The man stepped quickly back out of sight.

All the time Tom was talking, Nanny was working her way along. Tom wasn't sure he could make it clear around. There were some places a foot wide where the trail had crumbled away just since he had dug it out. He slapped Nanny on the rump to make her span those gaps, then mounted again. Many times his heart was in his throat as his gaze fell to the canyon floor. He could hear rocks and sand sliding down from the trail he was on. It could drop from under him. He kept watching back with his revolver in his hand, but he didn't think the men would venture far in single file. He would have all the advantage.

Tom's worry now was what he would do if he made it to the end of the trail. The men would probably go back by way of Hobble Creek. That would give him a head start, but Nanny was about worn out, for he had to ride her hard and treat her rough. If he tried to get his own horse the men would overtake him, and he did not want to lead them back to John's place.

When he was safely off the precipice Tom got down to see how badly Nanny was cut when he was forced to use his spurs. He was sick when he saw what he had done.

"I'm sorry," he said to her as he held her head in his arms and stroked her nose. He wished there were some way he could explain to her that he'd had to do it to save his neck.

As they worked their way down the mountain through the thorny thicket Tom sensed that something was lurking in the brush besides himself. He took all the shortcuts he knew because he was quite sure the men would not give up that easily; they would not want to let a witness to their dastardly scheme escape. He believed the men would follow the road and try to get back to where he was before he could get down off the mountain. They could do it with their fast horses. Whoever was in the brush now was not one of them unless he had been waiting there all the time.

Tom worked his way down to a thicket. He took off his spurs as he could walk with less noise, and in some places he could be seen above the brush if he rode the horse. He moved silently ahead now, leaving the horse where they entered the thicket. He wasn't taking any chances.

Tom hoped to get out of this without bloodshed but he checked his pistol to see if the chamber was full. He moved silently ahead now, pistol in hand, hidden by the brush. He met no interference. Then he heard the familiar nicker of a horse. Lying on the ground so as not to shake the bushes above his head and give away his position, he crawled forward. Peering through an opening, he saw the horse's legs. A smile crossed his face.

He rose from his hiding place and called, "John, it's me."

John stepped into the open, replacing his pistol in his holster. He hadn't been sure it was Tom. "Glad you made it back, brother. You sure had me scared."

"You had me scared too. I thought you were another cut-throat waiting in ambush."

"They will be after you, all right. We'd better not let any grass grow under our feet getting out of here. They are dangerous men to oppose."

"But how did you know where to find me?" Tom asked.

"That was easy. As soon as I saw you riding Nanny I knew

what your plan was. That was just about as risky as it would have been to shoot it out with them. You took an awful chance on that ledge. I hardly expected to see you alive."

"I've been in tight places before and got out," Tom said.

"Well you're not out yet. I knew even if you were lucky enough to make it around the trail you could never get away without a faster horse than Nanny. Let's go," John urged.

"Not until I turn Nanny loose; I left her back there, tied." Tom mounted his own horse and started to ride away. But John yelled, "No, you haven't time. I'll get her later. Besides, if they come looking for you and see your horse tied there they will think you're still in the brush and that will delay them."

They sped forward so fast that the Avenging Angels did not have a chance of catching up. It was a long time before they slowed down to speak to each other. They were almost at the main road now, and a decision had to be made.

"I sure hope Nanny gets well. I had to treat her pretty rough to make her lunge forward. You know how slow she is. But I think she saved my life. I cut her with my spur. The flies are bothering her pretty bad so get her as soon as you can. On second thought, you better send John Pants after her. They might wait there knowing someone will show up to get the horse and saddle."

"You're right, Tom. I'll take care of it, but I'm more worried about you than the horse. Your life isn't worth much if you stay around here. They'll get you, Tom, for sure."

"I know that now. Those men meant business. I've been wanting to go to California, and this is as good a time as any. I'll go to Dad's place tonight and wait around the blacksmith shop until a wagon train comes. I'll ride along with it."

"No, Tom, you must go now...today. Don't go back to the blacksmith shop. The Brighamites have their henchmen posted everywhere. Half the people in the little church here are either polygamists or in sympathy with their cause. Your saddle is packed and your rifle is tied there to your bedroll. We have given you half the powder. I feel it will not be long until we follow."

"I guess you're right, John. I'd rather stay here and fight it out, but it would only get you and Dad in a lot of trouble. Maybe I can find some of that yellow stuff out in California."

After they got down off the mountain, open space lay ahead.

they did not stop again until they reached the road. There was no one in sight in either direction.

"Well, John, I guess this is where I take off for nowhere."

"I'll ride along with you a ways."

"No need.... I'll make out."

"I know you will, but let's keep going. Those men will be coming down the road any minute, and we don't want them to know what direction we're headed." John led out at a full gallop.

They made long detours in order not to be followed, then worked their way across the marsh and forded Provo River. After they got on higher ground Tom looked back. He could see Springville and John's ranch. This was the first time he had felt sorry to be leaving.

They rode at a rapid gait for several hours. When they were up on the heights, they could see the smoke of Salt Lake City in the distance. At the place where Tom would take off across the salt flats they stopped to shake hands.

"Good luck, brother," said John.

There was so much to say that Tom said nothing.

John stood and watched until his brother-in-law had been swallowed up by the gathering darkness.

CHAPTER NINETEEN

Mary did not go to her father's as John had told her. There was work to be done; besides she had the gun, and Rover was constantly on guard.

Before dawn she heard someone coming and knew it was John because Rover had not barked.

He only told her that Tom was safe. He knew she had been up all night waiting. She looked so tired he would wait until another time to tell her Tom had already headed for California and they might never see him again.

He pulled off his boots and sprawled across the bed so tired he did not remove his clothes.

When it was time to feed the stock and milk Mary did not awaken him, but went herself to do the chores. Inside the barn it was still dark. She lit the lantern hanging in its usual place, then tossed hay into the mangers.

All at once there was a rattling at the outside door that led into the horses' stalls. She was frightened. Before she could think of what to do she heard a whinny and knew that it was Nanny.

Mary unbolted the door and let her in. As she removed the saddle she felt blood on it . . . then saw the deep gash in her belly. She got the lantern and more closely inspected the wound. She was angered at the sight of it. She wondered if John had told her all there was to tell. She hurried to the house and awakened her husband.

"John, John—come and see what has happened to Nanny! There is a big gash in her side, and I am afraid . . ."

"That gash in Nanny's side saved Tom's life," John interrupted. "Sit down, Mary. Now, I'll tell you about it." This time he did not hold anything back. For their own protection he believed she should know the exact state of affairs.

He told her how Tom had, in a daring feat, ridden Nanny onto the narrow ledge, thus escaping the scheme the Avenging Angels had contrived to get him alone in the woods, outnumbered three to one. He related in detail the events leading up to the attack—Tom's rumpus in Salt Lake City and the warning from the Moores. Mary was indignant because he had kept these things from her. "If I had known it I could have talked to Tom."

"No, Mary, it goes deeper than that. All Mormons are involved, and sooner or later I had to make my intentions known. This has made up my mind." John was deeply disturbed.

In September 1857, Captain Van Vliet of the United States Army arrived in Salt Lake. He entered the city peaceably, but the Mormons suspected he was there to make provisions for the oncoming troops.

When Brigham Young knew for certain that the soldiers were on their way he issued an edict ordering all members of the church to move into Salt Lake City and report for military duty.

John did not go. His reply to the church was that he would come after he had finished harvesting his crops and had sown the winter wheat. Without Tom's help they were longer in getting the last of the year's work done.

Winter was upon them before they were finished, but John still did not go to Salt Lake City to join with Brigham's troops. Neither did he plan for the next year's crops. He knew their only salvation was to leave the jurisdiction of the Salt Lake Church. To move off the land he loved caused him deep sorrow.

Some of his neighbors had already complied with the order and had gone into Salt Lake City to drill with the legion. So far none of them had come back. Brigham was getting ready for the approaching crisis with the United States Government. He needed more soldiers.

Another census was taken of all the people to determine which ones were loyal to the church. John was questioned again and again. He was given ample opportunity to change his views, but John was not a man to do so once he had made up his mind. Heretofore he would have been one of the first to carry out missions like taking the census, but he was no longer asked to take part in the business of the church, so he knew he was considered an enemy. Since the incident with Tom he felt he was being watched.

He was not only hurt but alarmed by the cold way he was treated by the officers, including Brigham, with whom he had worked in the church and whom he had so often willingly helped in the past.

Many of the Saints leaving the church because of the gap brought about by polygamy urged John to join them in their move to California while there was still time, but John was stubborn and stayed on. He knew full well the dangers that existed, yet he would not give in.

Then one night he was awakened by the barking of the dog. John rose and peered out the window. He could barely distinguish in the darkness the silhouettes of a number of riders. He heard them opening the gate to the barn lot.

"Who's there?" John called out.

"We are strangers and would like to buy some hay for our horses," was the answer.

John recognized the voice of Bill Smith, who he knew was an Avenging Angel. He drew back from the opening of the window and shouted in a commanding tone, "Get out of here, Smith, or we will give you lead instead of hay!"

John used "we" instead of "I" from force of habit, because Tom had always been there before. But the riders turned away, perhaps thinking Tom was there also.

John knew more incidents like this were bound to follow. He believed they had come to burn him out, as had happened to many others. It was no longer safe here. If he were alone, he would face it, but he did not want to expose his family to danger.

Mary hated to leave the land where they had toiled for five years, and which they had made one of the best-kept places in the community. Also, she hated to leave her father and Sally again after having urged them to come to Utah. She could not understand why they could not just pull out of the Salt Lake Church and stay where they were.

"There are gentiles here, and the church has not bothered them. Why should they be after us?" she asked John.

"Not us, dear, *me*," he answered. "The gentiles may ridicule polygamy, but they don't try to stop it. I do. I have opposed it in every way I know how."

John was silent for a few minutes. Then he said, "Now I know what I am going to do. I am going in there once more, as they have asked me to do, and I am going to state my beliefs, pure and simple, and tell them I want to be left alone. Then I am going to come back here and get to work."

Before dawn of June 18, 1858, John and Mary Griffiths loaded their two children into a canvas-covered wagon and headed north for Salt Lake City. They took with them a generous supply of food and water and what other articles they would need to live in the wagon for the next few days. John's saddle horse was tied to the endgate of the wagon, but Nanny and the two milk cows ran loose. It was Rover's job to keep them following close behind. Mr. Thomas would look after their stock until they got back.

There were many reasons why they wanted to make it to another farmer's place instead of staying overnight along the road. It wasn't that they feared an attack by the Indians, but because unexplained tragedies of all kinds were becoming commonplace in Utah these days. The cows slowed them down considerably, but the trip was completed on the third day without incident.

Mary was pregnant again, and the steady jolting of the wagon was very tiresome. It was a relief when the city loomed in the distance. They went straight to the Temple so John could report in, in answer to the many summons he had received requesting him to show his faith and goodwill by volunteering his services to the Legion.

The wall around that portion of the city took in several acres and included several big buildings as well as the Temple. It was made of mortar and rock and was eleven feet high. The entrance was a massive stone gateway, and as they approached it they could see armed guards stationed there.

This was a disturbing sight to John. The Temple to John was a sacred place and should not be profaned by the presence of armed guards. He was stopped at the gate. No one could enter without being questioned or leave without a pass. John could hardly believe that such a thing was happening to him in America. One of the guards knew John and simply asked if he had adequate camping facilities. The other one was a man John had met once while working on the Temple. This man either did not recognize him now or did not wish to. He inquired if John's wife and children were with him, and John replied that they were.

When he opened the gate the man announced to someone inside: "John Griffiths, entering; two children and one wife."

John knew that such an introduction classed him as an enemy to their cause. He had only one wife. The guard ushered them inside, and the heavy gates closed behind them. John wondered why there should be locks on the gates. It appeared that this walled enclosure was being used as a temporary barracks, for an officer of the Legion seemed to be in command. Although

John could not remember having seen him before he walked up to the wagon and spoke to John by name. John eyed him closely, wondering if he was one of the Avenging Angels who had tried to lure Tom away.

"Griffiths, you are here, I presume, to join the Legion?"

"No, sir," John answered.

"There are United States troops approaching Salt Lake City," the officer stated.

John pointed up to the United States flag that was rippling in the breeze. "I pledged allegiance to that flag. I don't intend now to shoot it down."

The officer angrily turned about and said to three men standing guard behind him: "Show this man where to put his wagon; then take the animals outside to the corral." Turning back to John, he gave him orders to remain inside the wall until further notice.

"That was not my intention. My wife has relatives in town, and we are going there as soon as my business is finished here." John showed his determination by holding the team in check when a man stepped forward and took hold of the horses' bridles.

By now twenty or more people had gathered around the wagon. A few were old friends and acquaintances, and fear clutched their hearts lest John should start a fight. Mary thought, Why can't John take an order just once without making a scene? She was afraid he would refuse to let anyone else care for the horses. She knew for sure he would not permit them to touch Rover, who was standing in front of the team with the hair standing up on his back and his teeth showing.

The man who had taken hold of the horses stepped back. Before John could decide what to do next, an old friend and neighbor of theirs, John Lewes, walked up to the wagon and said in an undertone: "Don't start anything, John. They are looking for an excuse to destroy us. Anyone who makes a false move or refuses to take orders is missing the next morning. Such men are secretly taken out in the night, and they are never seen again."

Mr. Lewes had climbed upon the wagon wheel. John motioned him aside so he could get down out of the wagon himself. But Lewes stayed where he was, still pleading with John.

"You heard about Brother Potter getting shot, didn't you?"

"No, I did not know about that. Are you sure?" John asked.

"Yes, I am sure. They also stabbed Parrish and murdered his son," his friend said.

"Oh my God, have they gone that far?" John said, aghast. Mr. Parrish had been a good friend. "That is a strong accusation to make against them, Brother Lewes, unless you are sure."

"I am sure; we are all sure. Ask anyone in here. It happened right at the gate. Our only hope is with the United States Army. We hear it is outside the city now and pray that it gets here in time to save us."

With a quick glance around, John realized that most of those being detained behind the wall were like himself—men who had openly campaigned against polygamy and had not volunteered to fight against the United States troops.

"I guess you're right," John said helplessly, looking around at the armed guards. He could see now that the situation was serious. Rebellion would only mean death.

John got out of the wagon and said submissively to the man waiting there, "Show me where to go, sir; I will lead my team myself." It was one of the hardest things he'd ever had to do. When he had driven in there, it had not occurred to him that as soon as his business was finished he would not be permitted to continue on his way.

It was hard to believe such an accident had befallen his friends. Both Mr. Parrish and Mr. Potter had been killed while trying to flee the city. There was no doubt in John's mind that they were after him, and he had foolishly walked into their trap.

He spent several days keeping out of the guard's way, just observing all that was going on. He came to the conclusion that if he was to get out of there himself and help others he must have freedom to move about, so he could find someone on the outside to help them. The only ones free to come and go without a pass were the soldiers of the Mormon Legion, so he decided he would have to become one of them to get the confidence of the guards. With that scheme in mind he joined the line of men waiting for enlistment.

John was issued a military suit, a rifle, and a saber, but no ammunition. He was ordered to report, in uniform, at another building. There he was asked: "Do you have a horse, Mr. Griffiths?"

"I had four when I entered this place. They were taken from me." Forgetting his plan, he spoke angrily. Again he was taken out of line and asked to remain inside the walled enclosure until further orders.

It was a disappointment not to be sent out with the other men, but he knew it was his fault. From now on he would have to control himself. John found it was true that the guards had orders to shoot anyone seen trying to escape, and more guards were stationed on the outside. It seemed to him that he was doomed to die. Now that he was clothed in the Mormon military uniform, the United States soldiers would shoot him, while without it the Mormons would shoot him. It would take cunning maneuvering to outsmart both.

"Did they force you into their army?" Mary asked when John returned to where they were camping by the wagon.

"No. I joined up myself." Seeing that Mary was confused, John explained his plan, then said, "You might as well get something to eat; we will be here for at least tonight."

They were there for many nights. John soon decided against trying to escape by climbing over the wall. That had already been tried and failed.

To realize the seriousness of what was going on, it was necessary to understand Brigham Young's position. He could be compared to a king who was being dethroned. Besides the fight in his church, the United States Government was claiming his Western empire. The Mormons had been moved out of the other states; there was no place left to go. Young was so frantic over the events taking place, John knew he did things against his own desires to try to save his own neck.

John was not given any freedom. He soon realized the Mormon uniform would do him no good. They knew that underneath he felt the same. So now he planned a much bolder plan of escape. He decided to offer a bribe to one of the guards. His reasoning was that if these men were low enough to shoot a man down because of his opinions on religion, they wouldn't be too scrupulous about making a deal with the other side.

John began talking to the guards and feeling them out. Then he decided which one was most likely to accept a bribe. He knew if this didn't work it would be all over for him. He made it as tempting as he could so the guard would not want to turn it down.

The Mormons celebrated Pioneer's Day on July 24. It was not likely they would celebrate this year because the United States soldiers were so close, but if they did it might be a good time to plan to escape. The first time John saw the guard he had picked, standing alone, he approached him and made his offer: clear title to forty acres of land, all fences and ditched, with good buildings and plenty of pure water, in Springville, bordering on Utah Lake, in exchange for freedom for himself and family.

As John had expected, the guard's eyes lit up. His mouth was thin-lipped with the corners drawn down—a symbol the world over which indicates selfishness. He told John they should not be seen talking together again. He would have a team and wagon and all provisions necessary for traveling to California waiting outside the gate at such time as it would be safe.

John did not tell Mary for fear his plan would leak out. On the day of the celebration he waited and watched for some word from the guard, but none came. On the evening of the twenty-fourth Mary was kneeling by the open fire, roasting a pan of wheat from which to brew their morning beverage. She whispered to John: "I have a message for you!"

He raised half up from where he sat as she continued, "There will be only one guard at the gate tonight, and it will be the one with whom you talked."

"How do you know this?" John asked.

"He was at the yard when I milked, and he told me to tell you."

"You spoke to no one else of this?"

"Of course not!" Mary was indignant because he had not trusted her.

John went to the wagon and examined the contents of the powder horn. To his surprise it was nearly full. He wondered how it could be, for he was sure he had not supplied it all. Without powder it would be hard to provide food and protection on the way.

John returned to the fire and knelt down beside Mary. The toasted kernels were giving off a pleasant aroma. Mary took from her bosom a slip of paper and handed it to John.

"The man said we are to come to the gate soon after midnight. The wagon will be waiting just outside. If anyone stops you, you are to show this pass and say that I am ill and that you are taking me to some friends. The man said he would be at the gate to let us through. From then on, we're on our own."

CHAPTER TWENTY

John and Mary spent the hours until midnight in anxious anticipation. He scolded Mary for telling the man who brought the wood for the people to burn that they would not need any.

"You mean I am to lie?" she asked, outraged.

"Please understand me, Mary; we are in a dangerous situation. Any little thing like that could give us away."

Mary brushed her hand across her forehead, saying, "I am sorry, John." And she was sorry. Very seldom did she snap back at him.

"I know our position is perilous," John continued. "Once out the gate I will not be able to help you. It will be safer with me walking alone and the children traveling with you. You realize, don't you, that we are risking our lives to get out of here? Do you still want to take the chance?"

"Yes," she said quickly, as if she had already made the decision. Then she added, "I have a feeling that if we don't get out of here you will be the next one missing. Ben Evans said if he got out of Salt Lake City alive he was going back to Wales. I almost wish we were, too."

"No, Mary, things were no better there. I know I will not find the freedom I am looking for by turning back."

They sat in silence for a long while. Then Mary spoke, "John?"

"Yes."

"What time is it?"

"It is nearing the hour. I have decided to make the walk to the outer gate alone," he said.

Quickly rising, Mary said, "No, I am going with you. I have everything packed and ready, and I have explained to Johnny that he is to be very quiet. I will awaken him."

"Don't do it yet, Mary. I keep thinking this might be a trap. I insist that I go first and see if there is a wagon waiting out there. If there is any shooting at the gate I don't want you and the children involved. I have enough on my conscience now."

"You might be hit yourself by a stray bullet," Mary said.

"If I am hit it will not be by a *stray* bullet," he corrected her. he did not kiss her good-bye; this was no time to give way to sentimentality. He slipped out of the wagon and disappeared into the darkness.

John's opinion was that there was only a ten-to-one chance he would make it back alive. He reached in his pocket to make sure he had the deed; it might be the one thing that would keep him alive. He knew he could count on the unscrupulous guard to help the highest bidder, and he was almost sure he had eliminated the danger that anyone had outbid him. The Brighamites would not pay more than that for his life.

He moved silently and cautiously, keeping away from any of the other camps. He resented having to sneak out on his friends, but he could not help them where he was. If he could free himself, he might get aid to them, also.

The moon had not yet come up, and only where there were smoldering fires or lanterns lit was there any light. Hearing movement to his left, he ducked to the ground and waited. It was useless to fight back if anyone was after him. John was well aware of that, but if a man is courageous he fights back against all odds. When he heard the noise again it was farther away. Probably a dog, moving about in the night.

When he started on he walked normally for he believed it would be less dangerous than skulking around trying to conceal himself. He had made half the distance when a man loomed out of the darkness. He must have been waiting there as John had not heard his approach.

"That you, Griffiths?"

John didn't answer, wanting to be sure it was the guard. "I come to tell you to hurry. There is a meetin' tonight celebrating Pioneer's Day. It will be lettin' out at midnight. I took my post a little early in order to get you out of here ahead of them. If you are out the gate just before they go through there will be so many rigs going away from here the other guards stationed around will think you are part of that crowd. Where is your family?" he asked.

"I had them wait in the camp until I was sure it was safe to go through the gate," John replied.

"You will have to go bring them now. There is no time to wait."

They both went back to the wagon and found that Mary had already awakened Johnny. She had given him a flour sack full of clothes, with instructions to hang on to them and to keep very quiet. He had managed to sling it over his shoulder, and it was nearly toppling him over. Mary had removed from the wagon and piled in a heap the things she thought they could not get along without. She had repacked and discarded items several times, packing into gunny sacks the most important of the lot.

When the men came up, Johnny was standing there with his heavy pack and Mary was holding the baby and John's rifle and powder horn. John no longer had the army rifle, as the Legion had requested its return a few days after it had been issued to him, but it was of no use without ammunition anyway. Mary knew John's rifle was ready to shoot; she had seen him tamp the load into it just before he went to the gate. She had thought he was going to take it with him then, but just before he left he had put it back into the wagon and had taken his pistol.

John explained to Mary that he had not got to the gate to see if there was a wagon waiting, and now the important thing was to hurry. The guard picked up the largest bundle, a covered canvas roll, like a roll of bedding.

He started right back and said to John: "You better carry the boy so you can get along faster. There could be other guards sent on as soon as the people start moving out. Some of them would know you."

"I thought I had a legitimate pass," John said.

"Some of them might wonder how you got it," said the guard.

John took Johnny on his back and picked up the bundle he had dropped. He grabbed another sack from the pile and started after the man, saying, "Come on, Mary."

But she went back to the pile, and, balancing the baby on her hip, frantically searched through the remaining sacks until she found the one she wanted. Picking it up, she started in the direction of the gate, but stopped after having taken only a few steps and returned once more to the pile of sacks. She searched until she found the one that was filled with the bread she had been baking for several days.

John stopped to see if she was coming, and Rover began jumping up to see why Johnny was not walking. The whole situation was very dangerous John knew. It wasn't what he had planned. He was at a disadvantage if he had to protect either himself or his family. What worse place could Johnny be than on his back if someone took a shot at them?

He put him down. Speed seemed now to be his only salvation. He took Johnny by the hand and started off again, moving as fast as possible. Still Mary was not coming. John grew exceedingly angry. He waited for her to catch up, and when he saw that the load she carried was what was holding her back, he grabbed one bag, tied it by the string to the one he carried, and slung them both over his shoulder. Then he snatched the other from her hand and threw it as far as he could "Now maybe you can keep up!" he said.

The guard was on the outside putting the bundle into the wagon by the time John and his family arrived at the gate. The gate was slightly ajar, and they cautiously pushed through. The first thing John noticed was that oxen were hooked to the wagon instead of horses.

"Where are my horses?" he demanded of the guard.

"I went to the corral but all the horses have been taken away," the guard replied.

"The agreement was that you were to have my cows and horses here and a good wagon."

"I did my best. I am sorry but the animals were not there. You best get started; the people will be coming. I will walk the hundred paces with you," the guard said. The agreement had been that John would deliver the deed to him one hundred paces outside the gate.

Mary began getting the children arranged in the wagon. She told them to lie down. She knew it was outside the gate where their friends had been killed. She barely got into the front seat when she felt the wagon moving ahead. She knew John was leading them. She sat stiff on the seat, watchful and silent, holding John's gun. She had made up her mind if the guard or anyone else shot John she would kill them.

It was impossible in the darkness to distinguish any movement around them. She listened for any sound of scuffling. After all, Mr. Parrish had been stabbed. Perhaps there would be no shooting.

It seemed an eternity before the wagon stopped. John was delivering the deed into the hands of the guard. There was a short wait while the guard returned to the gate. They heard the click of the lock and knew that he was back at his post, but they were not yet free.

John continued to walk ahead of the wagon in case anyone was waiting in ambush. He wanted to be out in the open where they could hear him walking so they would not shoot into the wagon where Mary and the children were. It never occurred to John that it was a heroic thing to do. Since his break with the church he had become accustomed to confronting grave danger. To remain alive one must have intrepid courage.

John took the advice of the guard and followed a road that led back toward some houses. If he were stopped before reaching them he could explain he was taking Mary there. From there he could take an old road that led back around the salt ponds and joined with the road to California. This roundabout way would take longer but seemed safer.

John goaded the oxen along at good speed. Mary, keeping her watch from the wagon, was still holding the rifle. They wanted to be as far away as possible before daylight.

Suddenly John heard a crashing noise beside the road. He drew his pistol and stopped the oxen. "Lie down in the back of the wagon, Mary," He directed.

The only answer was the click of the rifle being cocked. There was someone or something out there in the bushes. He half crouched beside the oxen and waited. Presently they heard it again, moving away through the bushes. It must have been a stray animal of some kind.

John smiled to himself as he thought of Mary and said, "Better pull the pin on that gun. I wouldn't like to be shot in the back."

He walked on, wondering if each step were bringing him nearer some trap. Or was he free again? Now in the deep darkness before dawn their pace was slowed, as he had to feel his way along. He dared not light the lantern that was hanging in the wagon.

As he walked, John could not help remembering the day he first entered Salt Lake City and shook the hand of Brigham Young. At that time he had thought: Here is peace and contentment; here I shall build my home. He smiled sardonically at the thought of how his dream had crumbled. His life and its little jokes! He must remember to laugh sometime, but now he must hurry on—his life depended on it.

It would take courage, faith, patience, and a great lot of strength to get over this hump. Perhaps it would take more than he had, for all of a sudden he felt so exhausted he could scarcely stumble on. He had walked many miles during the night, constantly prodding the oxen to keep them moving. How far he could not tell in the darkness. But there could be no consideration for human endurance; as long as the oxen were able to travel they must keep moving.

It was getting lighter now, and John climbed into the wagon for the first time. "If you can find a place to lie down there in the back, you had better get some rest," he told Mary. She did as he told her, never expecting to rest, because of her anxiety, but after a few minutes she fell asleep from exhaustion.

After a while John stopped to look back and see how far they had traveled. He beheld a gorgeous sight. The morning sun, not quite up, was throwing rays above the mountaintops, and the Temple was outlined in glowing orange. The beauty so impressed John that he declared anew his faith in God.

He sat there for a time meditating, held by its glory, until the sun burst over the horizon. Particles in the sand reflected the golden radiance, and all the earth seemed to be seething about it in the golden glow.

John was filled with a strange emotion, and he said aloud, "One man cannot destroy it." He decided then he would not give up the Mormon faith because a few radicals had taken it over, teaching false revelations and committing crimes concealed in the name of religion.

"We will join the Josephites and start anew," John solemnly asserted. He moved on without looking back again. It was as though a door had closed behind them.

CHAPTER TWENTY-ONE

Night and day had merged into a sleepless nightmare before John halted the wagon. He stopped by a cut through a sand bank that provided a small patch of shade. The oxen had begun to stumble and were a lather of sweat. John did not want to wear them out or have them become galled under the yokes when the journey had just begun.

When the wagon stopped Mary poked her head out from under the canvas top and asked anxiously, "What's the matter?"

"Nothing," John said. "The oxen are about worn out, and so am I. We will rest here for a while."

John untied the canvas covering from the water barrel that was fastened to the side of the wagon. Mary brought a dipper, and they all had a drink. It was cooler than the water in the canteen. Then John sparingly dipped out a little more, and, still holding the dipper in his hand, sank down in the shade.

"Would you get me a piece of bread to eat, Mary? I feel sick, my stomach is so empty," he said.

Then Mary recalled the sack John had snatched from her grasp and had thrown away the night before.

"Bread!" she cried. "Where might you expect me to come by bread?"

"I thought you baked bread for several days before we left," he said. He had been so long without a drink his voice sounded raspy. Mary saw how tired and sick he looked and was sorry she had spoken so sharply.

"Oh, John, it was the sack of bread you threw away last night."

"I didn't know it was the bread! At that time only getting out of there mattered. I'm sorry, dear," he said.

"There must be supplies in the wagon," she said and climbed into it with Johnny right behind her. He started digging into the boxes, too. As soon as he opened one thing he would toss it aside and open another, curious to see what was in them.

"Leave the things alone until I can go through them myself," Mary said to him. She found a large tin can filled with thick salted crackers, sprinkled on top with crystals of salt. She had never seen any quite like them before. They were not very palatable, but they ate them anyhow. It took all their ration of water to wash them down.

"What we don't need more of is salt," Mary said.

John kept his gaze on the road. One of the things that caused him concern, and one he had not mentioned to Mary, was the possibility that the guard who let them escape would also betray them. He might report them missing soon after they left. After he had the deed, it would be to his advantage to have John out of the way. As far as the guard knew, John might try to return to Springville. The guard could very easily report John missing and clear himself by saying John and his family had slipped through the gates with some of the other people who had passed.

After thinking over what might happen, he said, "You realize, don't you, if there is a fight it will be a matter of life or death for me and perhaps all of us?"

"If the Lord wills it, we will survive," Mary replied, trying her best to sound confident.

"God bless you, Mary. Always when I am about to give up you give me courage." He touched his rifle to be sure it was there. "I hope I will not have to use this, but I have a right to defend myself, and if need be I will exercise that right," he said.

"If they attack us, I know it cannot be helped," Mary said.

They rested only until the oxen were able to go on. Back on the trail they had to shade their eyes in order to see against the sun; its reflection on the salt-filled sand dazzled them. The dust the wagon stirred up blew into their faces, burned their skin, and made their eyes red. The heat was becoming unbearable; even in the morning it was near one hundred.

When they started on, John said to Mary: "Keep a lookout from the back of the wagon; if there is an attack it will help if we are ready for it."

"John, aren't you being overly cautious?" Mary asked. "I can't believe Brigham Young would permit harm to come to his own people."

"You forget, we are no longer his people. We are considered enemies. Do you want to return and proclaim yourself a polygamist?"

"You know better. But it is hard to distrust those you once loved and respected. At least I don't think they would harm the children. Do you?" she asked.

"Have you forgotten the Mountain Meadow massacre so soon?

Women and children were murdered there—and for no reason at all. We will not be dealing directly with Brigham Young, you know."

Mary moved to the rear of the wagon without saying any more and started to keep watch. Dust poured through the opening when she pushed the canvas curtain aside to look out. Soon there was a film over her and everything in the wagon.

"It does not appear to be His holy will to help us, leastways here on earth," Mary said pathetically. She had not intended for John to hear, but evidently he did because he shouted back at her from up front.

"Let us not lose trust in Him, Mary. Keep praying that help will come soon."

John let the oxen set their own gait now lest they play out entirely, and as the time passed they walked more and more slowly. Soon they were barely moving at all. The broiling sun was beating down upon them, and it was suffocating under the canvas top of the wagon. Mary wrung out wet towels and placed them on top of their heads to help keep them cooler. Johnny insisted on having a wet rag to put on Rover's head too. Besides the heat, one wheel had developed a squeal from lack of axle grease. It could be heard a long way off, but John did not stop even for that.

Finally they reached a chain of hills they had to cross. As they climbed a little higher out of the salt flats, there were patches of stunted sagebrush and hummocks of yellowish sand and bunches of high coarse grass. The oxen would not eat this but it afforded protection from the road. John decided this was where they would stop for a while.

After he unhooked the oxen and removed their yokes he cut off a bush, went back to where he had driven off the road, and brushed out their tracks in the sand. The light wind that was blowing helped him with this task.

John looked through the supplies and was glad to see that at least here the guard had not sold him short. There was plenty of axle grease as well as bolts and nuts and a few tools. But Mary was not as well pleased when she examined the food. The salt pork was mostly fat; the brown sugar was in hard lumps; there was very little wheat flour and no saleratus or yeast.

After John fed and watered the oxen sparingly he took his rifle and went higher up on the hill where he could get a good look around. He scanned the country for several miles back but could see no one coming. He was tired and hungry so did not go far. He hoped Mary would have something ready to eat by the time he got back.

Johnny and his little sister were glad to be out of the wagon. Mary cautioned them to stay close to where she was preparing the meal, fearing they might wander away and get lost. "Stay close to the wagon," she said. They went under the wagon and sat down where they felt more protected. The children could sense they were all in some kind of danger.

John, when he left, had hung his powder horn on the side of the wagon well within reach of little hands. Johnny saw it and took it with him when he went under the wagon.

On the way back from his walk John shot a rabbit. It would give them some fresh meat so they could save of their meager supply of food. He tossed it down at Mary's feet, walked over to the wagon, and reached for the powder horn to reload the gun. It was not where he had left it. His heart came up into his throat when he looked beneath the wagon and saw Johnny holding the powder horn up in the air with the cork out, pouring the last grain of powder out upon the sand.

"Johnny!" he screamed, but too late. "Come out here at once," John said sternly.

Mary dropped the rabbit she had started to skin and ran to the wagon. She knew by his voice that John was furious. Johnny was not quite four years old, but he knew it was wrong to touch either the powder horn or any of the guns. He had been warned many times and told that if he ever did he would be severely punished.

John reached for him but Mary pulled Johnny away. John looked angrily at her and said, "You must not question my judgment. Go get the dinner and mind your own business."

She released her hold on the boy when she saw the empty powder horn. "Forgive me, John," she said and walked away.

Johnny had been taught much about the powers above. "Ask the Lord to pick it up," he said to his father.

"We do not ask the Lord to do for us what we can do for ourselves," his father told him. Then he delivered a severe spanking to his son.

To be without powder was to be without food and without any means of protection. It was a frightening plight to be in.

After weighing it over in his mind, John asked: "What shall we do now? Shall we go on or try getting back to Springville?"

Mary did not answer.

"I don't believe you and the children would be fired upon if you went back alone. Maybe you could make it back to your folks. As for me, I couldn't expect to get past the first sentinel," John said.

"They want me out of the way too; I know too much about them now. We will go on to California as we planned," Mary said, starting to throw things into the wagon.

"Not so fast there. The oxen need a few hours rest, and I must put some grease on that axle before we can go on. You might as well cook the rabbit. I'm starving."

After they ate they tried to get some rest, but it was impossible to sleep with so much anxiety. Like fugitives they continually watched for someone to approach. Finally they decided that Mary would stay awake and keep watch while John slept.

Knowing there was someone watching, John was able to fall asleep. When he awoke it was already dark. A whole day had passed without an attack, but it could be they were purposely waiting until dark. The guard at the gate knew John was armed and would be a dangerous man to tangle with.

"You have been asleep a long time, John," Mary said.

"Have I? I didn't mean to sleep so long."

"Shouldn't we go on now?" she asked.

"I think not. Since they have not come before this, I look for a trap of some kind. They didn't let Potter or Bill Parrish escape, and I think they will try to stop us. They might have gone out the main road, not expecting us to come this long way around."

After a while John heard the oxen lie down. He thought to himself it must be midnight because the cattle usually rest about that time.

While they were stopped John fastened the sides of the canvas top up so the air could circulate underneath and make it cooler. Also, he could see out from all sides. It was so dark now he mostly just listened for sounds of someone coming. While he lay there waiting until time to go on his thoughts kept wandering from one thing to another. For some reason he kept thinking of his father. He remembered word for word the warning he had given him against the Mormons. If they were so ill-famed that their unethical ways had spread clear across the ocean, John knew now he should have heeded his father's advice. Under other circumstances he would have given it more consideration. He didn't mean to fall asleep but apparently he did, because when he next took note of the darkness the morning stars were coming out and the moon was well across its orbit. He arose quickly and woke Mary.

"Do you want something to eat before we start?" she asked.

"No. I want to get as far as we can before it gets hot. Besides, I don't feel hungry. You can fix something for you and the children on the way."

The country they would travel through now to the main road was irregular, with elevations here and there that afforded excellent hiding places—perfect country for an ambush. A light breeze was blowing that caused the few straggly bushes and bunches of tall grass to move constantly. In the half darkness it was hard to distinguish if someone was hiding behind them or not. Several times he stopped the wagon thinking there was.

All morning John had been on edge and alert. There was not a doubt in his mind that near where the roads met the polygamists would be waiting. He felt much like a soldier going to battle on his last day in the army; if tragedy was to strike, it had to be now.

CHAPTER TWENTY-TWO

As soon as it was daylight John began to stop every little while and scan the country in all directions. He was too nervous to sit still so he got out of the wagon and walked. At times he considered turning back—but where? He would prod the oxen on faster and faster until he was running to keep abreast, and then he would realize he was pushing them too hard and slow down again. He carried his rifle but had only salvaged enough powder from the sand to tamp one load.

They traveled a long way before the road started down again onto the salt flats. The sun was very hot, and they were all weary from riding so long in the wagon. John did not feel well; he had not eaten a bite since the night before. He spoke sharply to the children, scolding them for making noise or moving about in the wagon. They were so frightened they moved close to their mother and sat quietly. Mary knew his outbursts were caused by his love for them and his fear for their safety.

Finally John stopped and pointed out ahead. They were approaching the main road. It ran like a ribbon, east and west, as far as the eye could see. Going east it went straight to Salt Lake City. Although they could not see it from there they could tell by the high mountains behind it just where the city was located. After viewing every possible hiding place, John started on. He noticed the children climbing out from under the top onto the wagon seat.

"Keep those children down!" he screamed back at Mary.

"I don't like to frighten them needlessly," she said. "They won't stay down where they can't see out."

"Better make them stay down rather than have them be riddled with bullets! Someone can come riding down that road any minute."

Mary knew John must be sure of an attack to say a thing like that before the children. It was the most logical place, especially since it was the gatekeeper who had suggested they come this way.

When they were less than a half mile from the junction of the roads, John said, "I will walk a short distance ahead of the wagon now. Don't start until I motion for you to come, then keep that distance between us. Here, take the goad stick. You will need it to keep the oxen moving. If anyone shows up out there don't wait to see what happens to me—head the oxen toward Salt Lake City and keep going if no one stops you. You wouldn't have a chance crossing the desert alone."

He walked about one hundred feet, then motioned for her to come on. Mary knew John must be almost sick with fear, yet he walked on down the road into whatever danger might face them. She felt a deep respect for him, and sat up tall and proud to show him that she had faith in him.

Rover was with John, inspecting first one side of the road and then the other. Mary knew if there were anyone coming, even a long way off, Rover would give warning, so she kept watching him. She was glad they had not left him behind.

It seemed to Mary that this last half mile would never end. Then she saw John standing in the middle of the wider and more traveled road, motioning for her to come on. Years after she could still remember how he had looked, standing there in the middle of the road, smiling. It had been such a long time since she had seen him smile! It was as if a stone had been lifted from her heart. She eagerly climbed out of the wagon into his arms.

"There is no one here, John, there is no one here!" she cried.

They stood there a long time, John holding her tightly in his arms. "No, Mary, there is no one here. I do believe we have managed to escape," he said.

John looked around for signs of riders that might have passed that way recently. There were none. It was long past the noon hour, and he felt as if he could eat now.

"I don't see any shade so we might as well stop right here for lunch," he said.

John could not get over the feeling they were being followed. There might be a sniper waiting at the springs, he thought. They would have to stop there, and the Brighamites knew it. Also, they knew he would travel very slowly with oxen. Riders could easily overtake him any time they wanted to.

"You know, Mary, we're getting into Indian country now."

"I am not much afraid of the Utes that live around here, are you?"

"I wasn't thinking about the Indians themselves. Isn't it the usual way of the Brighamites to let their victims get into Indian country before they attack, then blame it on the Indians?

That's the way it was at Mountain Meadows, you know," John said.

Mary was now filled with optimism. When there was no one waiting at the junction of the roads she had made up her mind not to worry any more. So she didn't answer him.

Mary was sorry they had caused Johnny and May to be so frightened. She played with them now to erase their fears.

After they had eaten their meager lunch and were back in the wagon again, John said, "Mary, I wonder if you feel as I do, that we might be running into worse trouble than we are running away from?"

"What do you mean by that? Sometimes you say the strangest things."

"What I mean is that in our attempt to save ourselves, have we jeopardized the lives of our children?"

"You mean because of the heat? They are used to hot weather. At home they played out in it all day long," she added.

"There are many things we did not stop to consider. There is the danger of traveling alone in Indian country, and what if you get sick? I wouldn't know the first thing about taking care of you or a newborn baby."

He shook his head. His fears sounded even more serious when he spoke them.

"These oxen don't look so good, either. What if they play out? None of us would get far afoot. It must be 110 degrees out there in the sun."

"Oh, tut, tut!" Mary said. "You are just trying to borrow trouble! God knows we have enough without that."

"No, I am not trying to borrow trouble. I am just trying to determine where most of it lies, ahead or behind us. You know only what's behind, but I have seen the Great Salt Desert." He tried to tell Mary what it was like. "There are miles and miles and miles of salt, like a vast sea that extends as far as you can see, with the heat radiating off it like a hot stove. That is where we are heading, Mary."

"It has been crossed before, hasn't it?" she demanded.

"Yes, it has been crossed before. But that is no sign we can do it."

"I am not worried. Why can't we wait at the springs until this hot spell breaks or until someone else comes along we can travel with?"

"We will see," John said. He did not want to tell her just then, but he knew the hot spell would not break for weeks. They could not survive that long if anything should happen out there.

John noticed a board that had dropped from someone's wagon. It was warped and curled up from the heat, as if some giant hand had twisted it out of shape. He was not one to give way to despair, but he didn't know how to get them out of their predicament. He got out of the wagon and started walking again. It always helped him to walk.

Later he picked up a stone and threw it at a bird that was eating a dead animal. The blow killed it. He brought it back to the wagon where Mary asked with indignation, "Why did you kill that poor defenseless thing? I'll not cook it!" she exclaimed.

For the first time in weeks John broke into a hearty laugh, Mary looked so irate. He had not killed the scavenger to eat.

"I am going to make a bow and I need some feathers for the arrows. I never thought of anyone eating it," he said.

A little later they came to an outcropping of rock and huge boulders which formed sort of a ledge that afforded them protection from the hot sun. There was even shade for the oxen. John decided this would be a good place to stop for a while and rest. The farther away from Salt Lake City they got the fewer precautions they took. Mary no longer kept watch from the back of the wagon. This time they did not even get out of sight of the road.

"I wonder why it is that a pillar of stone gives one a secure feeling. There were times out there in that sand that I almost decided to turn back and fight it out," John said.

Johnny had become quite fond of one of the oxen. As soon as he got out of the wagon he went around and began petting him on the nose. "Mr. Oxen, don't you have a name?" he asked.

They had been riding for so long, John said, "Let's walk around awhile and get used to being on our feet. I can ride a horse all day, but riding in a wagon tires me out more than if I walked."

He wanted to see what was behind the rocks too, before he relaxed. They had just returned to the wagon and John was unhooking the oxen so they could rest when he thought he heard something.

CHAPTER TWENTY-THREE

John's first move was to grab the rifle, but when he started to throw the powder horn over his shoulder, his heart sank. For the moment he had forgotten it was empty. He wondered what he could do without a gun.

"Someone is coming!" he yelled. "Get out of sight as quickly as you can."

Mary automatically grabbed a canteen and ran with May toward the pile of rock, calling for Johnny to follow.

John dropped the gun and powder horn back into the wagon. He examined his pistol to make sure it was set to fire. He only had three bullets and wanted to be certain it was not set on an empty chamber; he might not get a second chance. Indians would understand gun talk better. John knew it was foolhardy to make a stand against such odds, but there was nothing else to do.

Within minutes the dust was rising from around the turn of the road, and John could tell it was a group, or at least more than one or two.

"Maybe it is the wild horses you told me about," Johnny said, loitering near his father.

"No, son, there is no mistaking the sound of shod horses. Go quickly with your mother."

"John, you can't fight that many. There is no use trying." Mary began to cry. The hopes she had built up only a few hours before came tumbling down.

"Do as I say, now. Get down behind those rocks and stay there!" he screamed at her. "I've got three bullets, and I'll get three of them before they can get me out of these rocks... and maybe more," he said, pulling a bowie knife from its sheath and sticking it in his belt. There was not a doubt in his mind that it was Brigham Young's hired killers.

When the riders saw John's wagon they drew rein and waited a minute for the dust to settle.

"Hey, Griffiths, is that you?" a kindly voice called out.

John had more sense than to trust a voice that sounded friendly. That ruse was an old one. He waited. They could not approach his hiding place without passing the crack in the rocks out of which he was peering. If it was who he thought it was he intended to shoot the first three that passed. Then he could die feeling he had had revenge.

Mary, in her hiding place, was busy trying to keep May from leaning out and exposing them. The rock they were crouched down behind was barely big enough to hide them. Johnny was not yet old enough to understand why his mother was crying, but he had certainly come to understand fear and to know when to lie still and keep out of sight.

John waited, motionless, holding the pistol cocked and ready. He knew with the wagon there in plain sight there wasn't a chance the riders would go on.

After a minute or two had passed Mary could not control herself any longer. She had to know who was there—Avenging Angels, bandits, Indians.... She peered cautiously from behind the rock. What she saw gave her a thrill of joy. Her prayers had been answered.

"John, John!" she screamed, running from her hiding place. "Don't shoot! It's the American soldiers."

The officer in charge dismounted and removed his hat as Mary approached. He noticed she was trembling from head to toe.

"Lady, we stopped to help you. Where is your husband?" he asked. Mary pointed to John, who had just stepped from behind the rocks, pistol still in his hand.

At the sight of the uniform of the Mormon Legioneers John was wearing, the soldiers, still sitting on their horses behind the officer, brought their rifles into place even before the officer gave command.

John lowered the pistol and, looking down at his garb, said, "I was forced to wear it, but I am not one of them any more. I am for the United States Government, sir."

The officer waved his hand and the soldiers lowered their weapons. The officer stepped forward and extended his hand. John holstered his pistol and reached forward, saying, "Thank God, we are safe. But what of the others we left back there in Salt Lake City?"

"The night after you escaped the United States soldiers scaled the wall and helped the others out. There was no bloodshed; the attack was made without resistance. All those that were held prisoner in Salt Lake City have been set free," the officers explained.

"How did you know about us?" John inquired of the officer.

"It was reported to our headquarters that you and your

family had disappeared. A Mr. Moore said he had received word from Springville that you and your wife and children had left there to go to Salt Lake City. As far as anyone knew you did not arrive. When it leaked out that people were being detained against their will behind the walled enclosure, Mr. Moore tried to contact you from the outside, to no avail. But when he saw your horse being ridden by someone else he was afraid of foul play and the first chance he got he reported it to us. Your friend is very worried. After those who were still being held in Salt Lake City were released we questioned them, but all they could tell us was that you and your family had been spirited away the night before we got there."

"That was how you knew my name then," John said.

"Yes. Just in case you had come this way we had orders to keep a lookout for you. We help anyone who is stranded along the road. There were several others who left Salt Lake City as soon as they could get away, and they are traveling along with us now," the officer said.

"Thank God, then there is still freedom and a government that will put down atrocities such as those that are going on in Salt Lake City!" John said with vehemence.

"By the way, Mr. Griffiths, just how did you manage to get away?" the officer asked curiously.

John told him. As he spoke he grew angry. He thought of his fields of grain, ready to be harvested, and declared, "I'm going to go back and demand the return of my farm."

"I wouldn't advise it if you are implicated as deeply as you say. Polygamy is a long way from being settled yet. I wouldn't be surprised if there is a skirmish before it is over. You know yourself Young is not one who gives up easily. As for your land, I expect the church will reclaim any place like that, and neither you nor the guard will get it. We are going to pull in over there on the other side of those boulders and wait for the rest of our outfit to catch up."

"We are most grateful for your company," John said.

"The moon comes up soon after midnight. We will travel by night and early morning until we get out of this desert country. Better be ready to move on the same time we do," he advised.

"I couldn't keep up with horses with these oxen," John replied.

"You will have no trouble keeping up with us. There are some supply wagons coming back there a ways. They are heavily loaded and must travel slowly. We riders scout ahead, sort of mapping the country, but we always get back to the wagons at night. You will hear the bugle when it's time for us to get ready to leave."

John thanked him again, but words hardly seemed sufficient to show his deep appreciation.

"How wonderful it is that we are still alive!" Mary said.

"Yes, indeed. Isn't it odd that so often when we ourselves can see nothing but evil, the Lord is preparing good for us? From now on I am going to keep in mind that God is always looking down upon us, and that all our sufferings will pass. Peace and trust will return whenever the good Lord sees fit," John said, his faith restored once again.

Hope sprang anew in Mary's heart as she prepared their meal. It was the first time in months they had eaten without the fear that it would be their last meal together.

As soon as the wagons passed over the last small chain of hills that had separated them from the great desert, the hot salt air hit them in the face. It had been hot before, but now the heat was like a blast from a furnace.

"I heard a man say once that coming onto this desert was like entering the gates of hell. I hope we will be able to stand it," John said.

The great white expanse extended as far as the eye could see. One thousand years ago the ocean had covered this region. It was sometimes referred to as a dead sea. An appropriate name, John thought. There were no desert plants growing to beautify it—nothing but desolation. It was like driving through an empty world.

As far as John knew there was no worse month to cross the desert than August. No one knew exactly how hot it was, but the people were warned to keep under cover. Even when the soldiers stopped for a short while, a few tents were hastily put up for shade.

For John, waiting under the wagons during the heat of the day was the most monotonous part of the journey. Even the children were noisy and quarrelsome. They lay on a blanket nearly naked; first one would make a loud noise and then the other. No one could get any sleep at all.

They were glad when it was time to start out again. At night the desert had a certain eerie beauty all its own. Under the full moon there was a creamy light, and it was so bright they could see the lines in the palms of their hands. A hot wind moaned softly overhead, and the night birds swooped down—owls and bats and hawks that made screeching noises in their flight for prey. Mingled with the desert noises were the sounds of the wagons scrunching through the salt. They could hear the canteens and gear hitting on the saddles of the soldiers traveling on ahead. John thanked God they were not alone.

On one occasion when John was in the company of the lieutenant he asked John: "Were you under any compulsion in Salt Lake City?"

"I learned it was not safe for me to object," John said.

"Explain what you mean. Who was the danger to come from if you objected?"

"From the Avenging Angels who were Brigham's hired killers. I presumed their orders came directly from him."

"Were you ever accosted by these Avenging Angels?" the officer asked.

"Indeed I was—enough so that I learned who some of them were." Then John told him about the narrow escape Tom had had and the time they came in the night. After John noticed the officer taking notes he was more cautious of what he said.

"Were these the same men who intimidated the prisoners in Salt Lake City?" the lieutenant asked.

"I never saw them there after the first day I arrived. Everything was done so mysteriously. Some of the men being held there against their will argued with the guards and tried to get away to go for help. First one and then another of these men disappeared in the night. Even their families didn't know where or when they went, and they never returned. We all thought they had been killed but could not prove it. It was rumored I was to be the next one missing. I left the same night."

"From what I have heard you are lucky to be here to tell the story," the lieutenant said.

"I have wondered how the attack was made against that barricade where the Mormons held us prisoners. Would it be against regulations for you to tell me?" John asked.

"Not at all. The attack petered out almost before it began. There was no resistance at all."

"I am glad to hear that. I would have hated to see any more innocent people killed."

"As soon as the people inside heard we had surrounded the place the prisoners climbed over the walls and the soldiers helped them down the outside. Not a single legioneer tried to stop them."

They had been traveling so many days John had lost count, but now they could look back and see the desert stretching for miles, and they could look forward and see mountains looming up in the distance—the source of their next water supply.

It seemed they would never get there, and then all at once Mary pointed at little tufts of withered grass growing in isolated clumps along the road. Soon dirt and sand were underfoot instead of the burning salt. They had crossed the great desert!

CHAPTER TWENTY-FOUR

The party of settlers and soldiers trekked on, day after arduous day, across the dry Nevada Territory. According to the map, they were getting nearer all the time to the most feared and treacherous place in Nevada country: the Humboldt sink.

There the river ended, forming a great sinkhole. At times it was a lake, but in late August it was a stinking, shallow pool, many miles long. Remains of old wagons mired in the mud were a grim reminder of the danger they would encounter.

All around the edges of the sink were dry alkali flats running out toward the swale. They looked firm, but in some places the top was only a thin, baked crust overlying a slough of mud. It would usually hold a man, but an animal stepping onto a soft spot would break through the crust to the slick slime underneath, slip, flounder, and mire down. If the wagons got stuck it was nearly impossible to get them out.

The soldiers made a wide circle around it, but sometimes they would come upon a spot where someone would break through and need assistance getting out.

Before they got past the Humboldt sink, John had a lot more respect for his oxen. He not only made it through the treacherous spots himself without needing help but with his oxen he was able to help others out. The oxen went at a slow, easy gait and were more sure of their footing than horses, and they did not panic as the horses did when they did get in such a spot. It was said that because of their split hooves they did not slide as easily either.

After leaving the Humboldt sink they had forty miles to go to the Truckee River. Now and then after they reached this river there were places being settled. As they traveled farther west they could see the tall peaks of the Sierra Nevada Mountains tipped with snow, and soon patches of green forest could be seen. After they got to the Carson River Valley there were beautiful fields of grass.

John was almost tempted to stop and start a farm, but by now he had California fever and he wanted to be completely out of any territory that Brigham Young claimed. The Mormons still considered Nevada part of their state of Deseret.

The most western trading post in Nevada was known as the Mormon Station. It was located in Carson Valley and well known to emigrants passing along the trail to California. The soldiers said they would make a brief stop there for the purpose of filling in supplies.

John and Mary learned that one of the men who operated the trading post was John Reese—the same man who owed Mary's father five dollars—and she intended to collect it. John objected, saying it had been too long, but she hunted up the letter from her father in which he had said he loaned Mr. Reese the money, and Mary could keep it if she could collect it. She had kept the letter tucked away in a little brown silk bag all that time.

As she started out to look for Mr. Reese, John said, "I don't think you should. You might stir up trouble. They might know about our problem in Salt Lake."

But she was determined. "He should not have borrowed money from Father and not paid it back. Besides, we need it."

To John's surprise, she came back with the money.

"Mr. Reese had not forgotten, but said he didn't know where to send it."

John laughed. "I remember Tom saying you would collect it if anybody could."

"Oh, I do hope I can find Tom as easily as I found Mr. Reese." She was anxious to see her brother. Not a word had been heard from him since the day he had fled the Avenging Angels. She hoped he was still alive.

They could tell by the unfriendliness of the people at the trading post at Mormon Station that the news had reached there ahead of them that the United States Government had taken over in Salt Lake City. They refused to sell to the soldiers. Their excuse was they did not have sufficient stock to supply the army, but they also refused supplies to the civilians.

"And to think Pa loaned that man five dollars!" Mary said indignantly.

They were told the next place to get supplies was twenty miles down the road. The California line was about halfway between. They went on, and the next day entered the state of California.

"If I had known before I left Wales what I would have to go through here in the United States, I might not have come," John said wryly.

Their first stop in California was Brannan Springs in Alpine

County. It was the first white settlement on the eastern side of the Sierras. Almost every wagon needed some kind of repair. The animals were getting thin because of lack of grass through the desert and alkali country. There was an abundance of feed here along the Carson River, and wildlife was plentiful. Hardly a day passed that they did not have wild game of some kind to eat.

There were several passes over the mountains. Carson Pass was the one most often traveled, but the Army was routed over Ebbetts Pass, a steep, hazardous route farther south. At the trading post they advised John to go by way of Carson, but he decided, in spite of the hazards, to stay with the Army.

The eastern side of the Sierras rose abruptly to the summit, and the road was narrow. In places it seemed as if the wagons would surely careen over the sides. John's wagon was heavy and cumbersome. It was satisfactory for crossing the desert but hard to ride in, jolting over big boulders and deep ruts. They were thrown from one side of it to the other side.

Mary was heavily pregnant, and the riding caused her such discomfort that she was forced to walk part of the time. John knew he would have to travel slower. At the first opportunity he told the lieutenant he was dropping out because of Mary's condition.

"No, Mr. Griffiths, not here. There is not a settlement between here and Murphy's. That old wagon of yours might break down and leave you stranded along the road. I think we are almost over the worst of it. I cannot permit it."

Once after a hard climb around a mountain of gray rock they came upon a tiny lake of deep blue, circled by flowers and fern. There was not room for so many to stop so they could only look as they passed by. Later they came to a larger lake where they remained overnight.

After starting down the west side of the Sierras they found the road was better, falling more gently over the slopes and through mountain meadows. Sometimes they traveled through groves of young fir and pine trees with open fields between where the grass was green and wild flowers of every kind and color literally covered the ground. Mary was excited when she found a flower like one that grew in Wales. Under the trees were lacy fern and moss-covered rocks, and even the fallen tree trunks were covered with velvety green moss. John declared he had never seen a country so beautiful since he had left Wales.

Water was plentiful. They crossed over many small streams and bubbling springs, and often they would stop and drink of the cool, clear water. It tasted wonderful after weeks of drinking stale water.

After a few more days' travel they began to catch glimpses of the Stanislaus River in the canyon below. Suddenly they entered a forest of giant trees so dense the sun could not shine through. They had heard of the giant sequoias, but they had not believed it could be true. Now they were looking at trees three hundred feet high and twenty feet or more in diameter. It was unbelieveable.

They were so impressed that the lieutenant stopped over for a night so they could all walk through the woods and look at the trees. While looking for a campsite they came upon an Indian camp. Up the hill from it was an outcropping of stone with deep holes in the rock where the Indians were grinding acorns into mash with pestles. Some were able to speak English and told them there was a white settlement a little farther on at Big Trees Camp. There were a few unpainted houses and a hotel for tourists coming to see the giant sequoias.

The last few days of travel Mary had a constant backache and was unable to climb in and out of the wagon without assistance. Her feet were so swollen she could not wear her shoes. The ride over the pass had been too much for her. During the night she took violent chills, and John was forced to go to the hotel and ask for help. He explained the situation to the night clerk and asked if there were a woman there who would come.

"There is none here that would know any more than you do yourself about delivering a baby," the man told him, "but there is a squaw at the Indian camp that is as good as any doctor."

John doubted it, but he had no other choice. He was grateful that the woman was willing to go with him right away. When he saw how the soft-spoken, gentle Indian went to work, he, too, believed Mary was in capable hands. She had no trouble in the dampness under the trees getting a fire going and water boiling. She had John help her lift Mary out of the wagon onto a bed of boughs so there was room to work around her. She took from her pocket herbs that she brewed, and soon after Mary drank the tea she was sleeping quietly.

John was disappointed that they had to stop. Only a few more days and they would have been at their destination, but he was afraid to take Mary on now. It would be risking her life as well as that of the unborn one.

John bade the soldiers good-bye and thanked them heartily for the help they had given him. Now that he had seen firsthand all the dangers involved in the trip across the desert and Nevada country, he was positive they could never have made it without the help of the troops.

John started working on a place to camp as soon as the soldiers had gone. He knew they would have to stay there until the baby was born and several days thereafter. He found a spot where Indians had camped and had left a temporary shelter of cut poles lashed together with strips of rawhide. John covered it with freshly cut boughs. The pine needles on the floor were clean and smelled good. John made a crude fireplace of stone to cook on and for warmth; it was always cool under the trees now that fall was in the air.

When John, with the children's help, had everything ready, shelves and tables and beds crudely nailed or lashed together of whatever material was available—bark, poles, rocks and a few planks that were in the wagon—they moved the supplies in. It was fun for the children and gave them a chance to look into boxes without their mother interfering. When everything was ready John carried Mary into the bough-covered arbor.

"Oh, it smells heavenly in here," she said.

It was good to be out of the wagon, even if they were only housed in a temporary shelter.

There was a small spring below the bank under the trees. John made a trough by removing the pith from a green sapling and sticking it into the bank where the water trickled out. It made getting a drink or catching a bucketful easier. This so intrigued the children they spent most of the day going to the spring to drink from the spout.

After a few days of rest Mary was relieved of her fever and nausea. As soon as she was able to be up she let the Indian woman go, thinking she would be all right now for a while longer. She hoped that in a few days they could travel on to Angels Camp where most likely there would be a doctor. John hoped so, too.

They had been forty-three days on the road, and often there

was not enough feed for the oxen nor enough time for them to graze. They had been constantly goaded on faster than was their natural gait in order to keep up with the soldiers. Now they were in poor shape. One had a galled spot on its neck caused by the constant rubbing of the yoke. So, after their own needs were taken care of, John turned his attention to getting the oxen back into condition.

After applying soft pitch from a pine tree to the sore on the oxen's neck he herded them back up the road to an open meadow to feed. John had to stay near for fear they would wander away or be stolen by someone going through or by Indians who often thought any animals running loose were theirs for the taking.

Mary was expecting John to return soon for dinner. She stood stirring the contents of a large iron pot suspended from a forked stick over the burning end of a small log stuck lengthwise into the fireplace. It was more of a young tree than a log, and the shriveled brown pine needles still clung to the branches, waiting to be fed to the flames. May was playing on the floor.

Suddenly the little girl gave a loud wail when a splinter pricked her bare foot. Mary turned quickly and bent over the child just as the dried branches flared into a blaze. It caught the tail of her long, full skirt as she bent over and drew it into the fire.

Mary grabbed up her skirts and ran from the improvised shelter so as not to set fire to it and burn the children. By now her loose blouse had caught fire and she was a flaming torch. She ran toward the spring screaming, "John, help me! John!"

CHAPTER TWENTY-FIVE

John was nearing the camp with the oxen when he heard his wife's screams. He came as fast as he could run. First he dashed into the shelter. Only baby May was there, lying on the floor crying.

John knew Mary would never leave the baby unless she was forced into it. He picked up May and ran outside again. Mary's screaming had stopped, but he saw Johnny standing on the bank above the spring screaming "Mama! Mama!"

The thought of renegade Indians flashed through John's mind as he ran toward the spring. Then he smelled burned cloth and flesh, and was soon where he could see Mary lying prone in the mire by the spring. The Indian woman had reached her first and was kneeling beside her, covering the burns with cool mud. Mary's outer skirt was lying there, still smoking; only the belt and a few shreds were on her body. The back of her calico blouse as well as the homespun underblouse which all married Mormon women wore had been consumed by the blaze, leaving her back exposed. It was a solid mass of burned skin, and where she had rolled over briers and hard objects in the mud, the skin was broken and oozing blood.

John was faint with horror at what he saw. He fell to his knees so if he did pass out the baby in his arms would not be hurt. He gently put May's hand in Johnny's and ran to Mary. She was conscious but because of the pain, she was unable to speak or move. She was in a state of shock.

"Speak to me, darling, speak to me!" he pleaded.

She made only faint moaning sounds. He tried to get her to look up, so he could see how badly her face was burned. She was lying on one arm and he could see that the backs of her hands and arm were badly burned. He prayed she had saved her face with her hands—but it would not matter how badly disfigured her features might be if only she lived, he thought. He wanted to carry her back to the shelter but she screamed with pain when he touched her.

The Indian woman said, "No move lady. I get help."

She waved her hand and several Indians came into sight with a stretcher that had been made by lacing rawhide around two long poles. They eased Mary gently onto the stretcher, carried her face down to the shelter and placed her on a piece of clean white cloth John had thrown across the bed. The Indian woman took over. John just stood there, unable to think what to do. Tears ran down his face. He could not even pray.

Johnny held onto his little sister. He knew it was what his mother would want him to do. May was afraid of the Indians, so she did not try to pull away.

Even in her agony, Mary thought of her children. Finally, she raised her head. Thank God she could see! She looked into the terribly frightened face of the little boy standing beside her bed and tried to reach her hand to him but could not.

"Johnny, Mama will be all right," she whispered. "Take sister outside and stay with her." Johnny looked relieved and did as he was told.

As soon as John heard Mary speak he came to her. He fell to his knees and thanked God she could see. Mary had kept the front of her clothes above her waist from burning by clutching them tightly over her face and head. Even though the blaze from her outer skirt and apron had been burning her hands she had never let go, knowing she must protect her face and eyes. The heavy woolen petticoat she wore had protected her from her waist down.

"Get some boiled water and clean the dirt off me and, John, hand me my consecrated oil," she ordered. It was all she could do to keep from crying out in pain but she remembered the frightened look on Johnny's face and only moaned quietly.

It seemed as if the huge pot filled with water would never boil, and when it did they had to wait for it to cool before they could wash away the charred clothing sticking to her back and shoulders. She was covered with mud from rolling over and over in the mire by the spring to put the fire out. The burned places were now forming great blisters. Because there was no other disinfectant Mary told them to add a small amount of salt to the water.

John worked ever so gently, but at the first application Mary fainted. The Indian woman pushed John aside. "Clumsy," she said. John watched her skillful fingers as she worked. She moved quietly about in her moccasined feet. As she pressed a cold cloth to Mary's face John noticed a faint odor of herbs to it.

Mary looked at John, a steady, fixed gaze with wide-open eyes.

Then all at once, her body tensed. There was a silence, then the squaw said to John: "More hot water, quick! Baby come now!"

John refilled the big iron pot and raked the hot coals around it. Then he remembered Mary had told him several times that there were clothes and a blanket for the baby tied up in a linen tablecloth in a chest, still in the wagon. He found them and laid them out, ready. Then when there was nothing to do but wait, he began to get panicky.

He went to look at Mary. It had been a long time since she had moved or made a sound. Her face was as white as the pillow she lay upon; to John the pallor of death seemed evident. He touched her face and it seemed cold. His nerves on edge, he ran out into the open air.

His first thought was to pray, but with bold defiance he didn't. How could he ever reach the Lord when he felt such bitterness in his heart? He recalled how many hours he had spent kneeling in prayer and his faith had been firm, yet God kept dealing out tragedies to him. To take Mary from him would be without reason.

In the face of so great a sorrow John renounced his faith and rejected any comfort that might come to him through prayer. He stood gazing up at the sky as if he were trying to receive some assurance from the great beyond even while he blamed his Lord. Then he started walking through the forest without direction. He walked faster and faster while he labored with his soul.

With this exertion his sanity returned and he began to feel remorse. Not only had he turned his back on the teachings of the Lord, he thought, but he had walked out and left his son and infant daughter who most needed him now. He must return quickly to care for them. But first he knelt where he was, deep in the forest, and asked God's forgiveness. When he arose his delirium was over and he resolved that, even if Mary did die, he would go on for his children's sake.

He had walked a short distance from the spot where he had been kneeling before he began to fear he was lost. He looked around, trying to get his bearings when he saw a movement in the brush. Then an Indian stepped from behind a tree and started toward him. "Squaw say tell Mormon that white woman be all right now."

"You mean my wife is alive?" John asked.

The Indian nodded his head.

"Thank God," John said humbly. Then, to the Indian, "Lead the way, for I do not know where I am. I was lost in both body and soul."

Over and over Mary thanked God that her eyesight had been spared and her face would not be disfigured. Unlike John, she had not lost faith. She asked blessings for her husband and her two living children. She did not mention in her prayer the baby that did not live. With her implicit faith in God she accepted the double tragedy.

By the time John got back it was afternoon. The children were taking their naps. Mary was sleeping. The Indian woman was washing clothes. She told John to leave Mary alone, and he knew she had given her something to make her sleep.

John looked around and saw the baby was not there so he knew it had not lived. The next day she showed him where she had put it. John felt very grateful to these friendly Indians who had helped them in their time of need. The man who had followed him into the woods offered to help him with the burial of the child, but John wanted to do it alone.

As soon as the people at Big Trees Camp heard of the tragedy they came to offer their help. There was nothing for anyone to do now; the Indians had done it all.

The next day when John returned from feeding the oxen he was surprised to find Mary propped up before the fireplace with her back toward the open fire. The Indian woman pointed at her and said: "Fire draw fire; good to heal bad burn."

It was torturous treatment, and tears ran down Mary's face, but she followed the Indian's instructions. It was incredible that after a few such treatments there was not nearly as much pain, and her back was less red.

It was many days before Mary was able to move without pain. She could not wear any of her clothes that fastened around the waist. Instead she wore her long white nightgowns day and night, and if anyone came she wrapped up in her big shawl.

John began to worry about the weather since winter came early in the high Sierras. Most of the white people were moving out of Big Trees Resort, and the Indians were preparing to go back to their winter quarters. It was damp and cold under the trees. Because of an early rain John was forced to remove the canvas top from the wagon and use it for a roof in place of the boughs.

Mary's hands, though burned badly, healed quickly. As soon as she could hold a needle she started sewing on some calico. One day she held it up to show John she had finished a long full dress that she could wear over her nightgown. Now she had something to wear, and she believed if they traveled slowly she could stand to go on. She was anxious to leave this place with its painful memories. Also, provisions were getting low. She decided they must get away. It would be weeks before her back would be well, but they could not wait that long. There was danger of being snowed in. They would have to start even if they traveled only a few miles a day.

John put the canvas top back onto the wagon and loaded their belongings. Early the next day they moved down the mountain. Mary looked back through the gray morning mist at a tiny grave over which a cross had been placed. The name "Frankie" had been carved upon it.

CHAPTER TWENTY-SIX

In the latter part of October 1858 John, Mary, and their two children drove into Angels Camp, Calaveras County, California.

Angels Camp was like all mining towns—hastily built, without plan or design. Each builder had his own idea, but uppermost in his mind was the desire to build quickly in order to start selling his wares.

John traveled slowly along the street past the big Calaveras Hotel, where men were still working on the upper story, then on past Stricklers general merchandise and saloons and other places of business. Through the open doors and windows Mary could see colorful granite buckets and pots and pans. There were shiny tin cups wired together hanging beside the familiar iron kettles and big frypans. A barrel outside the door was filled with mops and brooms and all the things a woman needs to keep a house clean. But when they passed a store with yards of bright-colored gingham and calico draped inside the window Mary could stand it no longer.

"Oh, I wish you would stop!" she burst out. She wanted so much to look inside the stores. She longed to have a house again. It was a mean thought but she felt she would not be very sorry if the oxen did give out so John would have to stop here and get a job.

They had noticed that Tom, the ox that had seemed the stronger of the two, was slowing down. This morning he was still down when John went to bring them in, while ordinarily he would have been up eating by that time. John did not want to spare the money to buy a team of horses, and he did not know of any place where he could buy another ox. It would look funny to have one horse and one ox hitched to the wagon.

"By traveling slower and stopping more often maybe Tom can keep going for a while longer," he said.

At the end of the street they came to a public watering trough and a place where they could leave the wagon for a while. John jumped to the ground from the high wagon seat and turned to help Mary. She handed him the little girl, and then he helped her down. Johnny climbed out the other side.

It was easy to tell their outfit had traveled a long distance. Those who had seen them coming into town began to gather around. Often travelers coming from afar carried mail.

A man came forward, reaching out his hand, and said, "Howdy, strangers. Where you from?"

"Salt Lake City," John replied.

"Ya' all didn't cross that devil country this time of year, did ya'?" he asked.

"Yep," John answered while he unpinned the yokes from the oxen.

"Well, by the gods ya' must be hell for punishment. Come on in the saloon and I'll buy ya' a drink."

"Thanks, friend, but what I need most is a good drink of water. I'll get it here at the trough and at the same time let these poor bulls have one." He led the oxen to the water, then they all had a drink of water from a pipe that brought a continuous stream into the trough. Mary washed the children's hands and faces, then started down the walk toward the stores.

John found a shady place and tethered the oxen. He told Rover to keep watch at the wagon, then followed. He stopped to seek information so often that he reached the store as Mary was coming out.

"I am going down to the hotel and read the register. Might be somebody registered there we knew one time or another," John said.

Mary knew he was looking for Tom. "All right," she said. "I'll go back to the wagon with May. You take Johnny."

John and Johnny were gone a long time. Mary was getting awfully tired waiting for them to come. Since her accident she'd been easily disturbed. John had a paper in his hand and was smiling. Her first thought was that he had news of Tom.

She went to meet them. "Did you find Tom?" she asked.

"No, but I have a job."

"Here?" Mary asked.

"Yes. It seems we arrived at just the right time. A Mr. Hamlin was in the hotel lobby, hiring men. When I told him I was a family man he not only hired me but gave me a subcontract, so I am my own boss. He said he was tired of hiring drifters who would stay with a job only a few days and then quit."

"What kind of job is it?" Mary asked.

"Mr. Hamlin has contracts from several different places to furnish rails and stovewood. It is an all-winter job, and I'll get paid according to how much I get out. Sounds pretty good to me."

John saw to his surprise that Mary did not appear to be very happy about it. All the way through the mining country she had urged him to stop and find a job. He had taken this job only because of her.

"Aren't you glad about it?" he asked.

"Yes, I am glad you have a job...we need money. But I thought we were going to live in a house."

"Perhaps you will like it better when I tell you he also furnished a house for us to live in."

"You mean we can move into a house?" she exclaimed joyously.

"Right now if you want to. It's just down the road a ways," he said pointing.

It did not take them long to yoke the oxen and start in the direction of the house. On the way Mary visualized all kinds of houses, but she wasn't prepared for what she saw when John drove into a treeless, rocky yard, and stopped beside an unkempt, unpainted, dirty shack. Even John was disappointed, but he said in a cheery voice, "Well, this is it."

"I would as leave live in the woods as in that dirty hovel," Mary said vehemently.

"Well, what did you expect for a woodchopper's wife?" John only meant to tease, but Mary began to cry.

"Oh, come now, it's not as if we were going to live here forever," John said.

Johnny was already running through the house, yelling for his mother to come and look.

"Mamma, there's a stove," he said.

They entered and found that Johnny was right. There was a cookstove as well as a homemade table and bench. The place was as dirty inside as out. It was littered with straw from bunk beds, and there were chips all over the kitchen floor where someone had chopped wood in the house. They could tell it had been occupied recently from the odor of stale food in the air. There was a can of rancid grease on the back of the stove and eggshells and orange peel under it.

"Looks like some of Mr. Hamlin's woodchoppers have been batching here," John said.

He went outside, picked up a stub of a broom he had seen in the yard, went back into the house, and started sweeping.

"You all clear our of here while I clean this place up," he said.

"I think I can do it if I take my time," Mary said.

"No, you cannot. You are in no condition to be in here in this dust and dirt. You will have enough cleaning when I get through. All of you clear out now!" He was already throwing things out the door.

Mary knew he was right. The worst thing that could happen to her now would be to get infection in the still unhealed burns on her back. She rested in the shade of the wagon until John called out, "It's all yours now. I will go and inspect the well and bring you some scrub water." The children followed him as he left the house.

It was a dug well with a box built around it, but there was no cover over the top of the box. John's first thought was that he would find some boards to put over it before one of the children fell in. There was a windlass to hoist up the water, and the rope was coiled around it with a leaky bucket attached to the end with a harness clasp.

John turned the windlass backward by hand to let the bucket down. Then he drew up the water and set it down where Rover could get a drink. He told the children not to drink until he could test it. He found a clear bottle and washed it clean. Then having filled it with water, he held it up and looked through it toward the light. The water he could see was clear and smelled sweet.

John filled everything that would hold water and carried it to the house so Mary would have it for cleaning. He knew she would scrub everything in the house, even the walls, before she would allow them to move into it.

They started to go in, but Mary said, "I don't want the children in here yet. It's so dirty and there is broken glass all over. Keep Rover out, too." John knew that meant him as well.

"I don't see how the children can get any dirtier than they are already," he said, and knew the minute he said it that it was the wrong thing to have said.

"Well, can I help it? Everything they have touched since we got here is dirty," Mary said in defense.

"If you can get along here by yourselves for a while I would like to go back to town and find out more about where I am to go tomorrow and how I will get there."

"We can manage," she said.

John started out, but as he passed the wagon he stopped and

called back to Mary, "Do you want the grub box and cooking stuff brought in there from the wagon?"

"No, not yet. All I need in here now is a scrub broom and plenty of soap and water," she said.

"Don't try to do it all at once. I will help you when I get back," he assured her and started off to town.

"Don't let the children go near that well," he called back.

CHAPTER TWENTY-SEVEN

When John got back to the hotel Mr. Hamlin was still there.

"I didn't understand when I talked to you before just where the timber is located," John said.

"Since you don't know this country it will be easier if I pick you up in the morning and show you where it is. Say about seven," he suggested.

John said that would be fine. Then he went out to inspect the town and to talk to anyone who was so inclined. He was most anxious to find out all he could about California farmland. So far, except for a few hidden valleys, he had not seen any land that looked productive. No one he talked to seemed interested in anything other than mining.

All of the settlements in the Sierras had sprung up because gold had been found there, and Angels Camp was no exception. In 1848 Henry Angel and a man named Carson found gold there in the creek and the mining operations were built right on the spot. The town grew up the hill from it like spreading fire. Ten years later it was still booming.

John wondered if a new strike had been made, but he was told that the neighboring town of Columbia had been wiped out by fire because of the lack of water. Many of the merchants, businessmen, and families were relocating in Angels Camp because of the abundance of water from the creek. John realized now how lucky they were to have found any kind of house to live in.

Both Mr. Angel and Mr. Carson had found the gold that started Angels Camp, yet John noticed that the name Angel was used more than Carson. Angels Creek, Angels Camp, Angels Rooming House, and even Angels Beer Hall! Almost everyone John talked to offered him a drink. It was different than anywhere in the state of Deseret, yet the town seemed orderly enough. He was told that Mr. Angel had imposed strict rules on the miners in order to insure law and order.

When he got home he was surprised to find Mary cooking over a bonfire and preparing supper on a table outside.

"Why are we eating out here when we have a house to eat in?" John asked.

"I got so tired I could not scrub any more, and I just

can't eat in there—where mice have been in the cupboards—until the whole place has been washed out," Mary said.

They slept that night in the wagon, but it was a deep, restful sleep since they knew they had a house and a job and were safe from harm.

Long before daylight, John was up. He had many chores to do before Mr. Hamlin came by to take him to the timber. He filled all the buckets and tubs with water from the well so Mary would have it for cleaning the house and washing. He also prepared his own breakfast.

In the mornings it was very difficult for Mary to move. During the night the burns would draw up and crust over; then when she moved the sore places would break open and bleed.

Every morning and night John applied olive oil to her back to make the skin more elastic. She did not get up when John did but stayed in bed as long as the children slept to give the oil a chance to penetrate and soften the skin.

On this particular morning she could not sleep but lay there thinking about the home they had left in Utah, the green fields and the lake which she had loved. What a price they had paid to be free! She thought of her family in Springville and wondered if they were well. And Tom—it was not likely he was even alive.

Mary knew she must start making the house livable. She wanted to make it as clean and nice as she could before John got home, so she spent the whole day fixing it up.

Coming home after work John could see the smoke rising from the crude chimney, curling upward into the sky. It looked homey and peaceful. He was tired, but it had been a profitable day and he was happier than he had been for a long time. He was having to begin all over again but that, too, held a certain fascination. At least he was again free to act as he chose. Here in America liberty was not a dream, even if sometimes he did have to fight for it. To John it seemed a blessing from God to have a job, food, a roof over their heads—and just to be living at all!

As he neared the house Rover came to meet him, walking with a prancing gait as if he felt a certain pride in having a house to protect again instead of just the wagon. John stopped long enough to pat him on the head. They had been through a lot together.

When John entered he could see that the house shone. The aroma of freshly baked bread, pork, and beans filled the air. Mary came from the other room. She was so weary she could hardly stand, but there was a look of accomplishment in her eyes that had not been there for a long time.

John had worked until nearly dark and then walked two miles to get home, so it was late. The children had already eaten and were in bed. He hurried to get washed up while Mary served their dinner on the table that had been left in the house. She had scrubbed it with lye water until the pine wood looked almost new. Even though they were using powder boxes for chairs it was good to be able to sit at a table and eat. Without interruptions from the children, they sat over their meal for a long while and talked about many things.

Now that they had an address they decided the first thing they must do was to write to their parents. It had been a very long time since John had heard from any of his family in Wales. Mary was concerned over the welfare of her family in Springville and most anxious to know if they had received word from Tom.

John took pen in hand, but he hardly knew where to start. Things had not come out as well as he had anticipated. He hated to admit defeat, yet he did not want to misinform his parents, or they might want to follow in his footsteps. What the situation in Salt Lake City would be after the United States government took over was something he could not foretell. It was difficult to explain to anyone who did not understand what had taken place there. He did not want to condemn all Mormons, yet the outlook was not good under the reign of Brigham Young. He paused for a long time between sentences, rubbing his head thoughtfully. Mary had her letter finished before he had hardly begun.

There was still no daily mail route to Angels Camp. Several different means of mail delivery had been tried, but all had failed. Often it was carried by special messenger or travelers. Other mail came haphazardly by stagecoach from Sacramento. It was left in a box at the hotel. Those who were looking for messages went there and looked in the box themselves. Sometimes mail would remain in the outgoing box for a week or more before it was picked up. Letters that arrived had often been written months or even a year before, depending on where they had come from.

John's wages were paid in gold; he believed at times it should have been more, so he purchased a small set of scales and carried them with him when he was to be paid or when he was going to buy or sell anything. He took them with him when he went to buy the horse which probably saved him many times the price of the scales.

The weather was growing cooler. Some mornings it was so cold John's hands grew numb, and he could hardly swing the ax straight. He did not earn much, and he finally got so discouraged he quit. There were lots of jobs available and on January 25, 1859, he went to work for Charley Shedrick for two dollars a day. He drove a team hauling rails.

It had been nearly three months since Mary had sent the letter to her father. She went to the hotel every day and looked into the box, hoping for an answer. After many futile trips she came home one day in tears.

"I want so much to hear from Father," she said.

"I know you do, but you must make up your mind that the children and I are your family, and if you never hear from anyone else we will get along by ourselves—and happily, I hope. You must do it for the children's sake," John told her.

"If only we knew what happened to Tom," she said.

"Eventually you will hear from your father and as for Tom, we might never know. I can hardly believe he came all the way to California without leaving a trace behind him. I have become convinced he never got out of Utah. The Avenging Angels must have caught up with him. I should have gone with him, but as usual I bungled things. You should have stayed with your father," John said.

"None of it was your fault, and my place is with you. I have not given up hope. I have a feeling Tom is still alive," Mary said. She dried her face and started to cook dinner.

"I wish you would quit going to look for mail. From now on I will stop and see if there is any. This watching and waiting is not good for you in your condition." Mary was pregnant again.

"I will try not to let it bother me. I forgot for the moment that the Lord is looking after us," Mary said.

"One of the good things about our marriage is that we never both lose faith at the same time," John replied.

CHAPTER TWENTY-EIGHT

The letter finally came. John, arriving home from work one day, handed it to Mary.

"Read it aloud," he said, eager to hear what it said himself.

Mary's hands trembled as she broke the seal. It was written in Welsh on a large double sheet of blue paper. Mary read:

Dear Children, John and Mary Griffiths,

Received yours dated Nov. 18, 1858. All in good health. I can't describe the joy I felt upon receiving your letter after having been expecting it for such a long time. Many a time I thought you had been killed by the Destroying Angels or something else, but I am glad that you arrived safe in the free country. I have but little news at present. The United States Court has started in the City but not much has been done. It is said that Brigham has been fined $50,000 dollars for unlawfully jailing one of the drivers and held one or more of the Angels, nothing has been done here yet. Soon a court will be held in Provo. The Angels are afraid and trembling. We have sold the sheep for $7.50 each and . . .

"For heavens sakes, why doesn't he say something about Tom?" Mary stopped to say.

"Read on, read on," John said.

. . . sold a load of wheat for $1.75 a bushel and bought a yoke of oxen and two cows. It would be easier for you to induce me to come there than go to the States. We think we will stay here another winter. The weather is very cold here at present. . . .

Mary turned the page over, stopping to wipe a tear. It seemed obvious that her father had had no word of Tom either. Then suddenly she cried. "It's a letter from Tom! He is all right! He is all right!" She could no longer control herself. Tears were streaming down her face.

John grabbed the letter and noticed the different handwriting on the back of Mr. Thomas's letter, and started to read.

Dear Brother & Sister

After quite a separation . . . I take my pen in hand to write to you, hoping you will receive them . . . the scene I saw when I returned home . . .

John was so anxious to find out how things were he sometimes read aloud—skipping lines and sometimes mumbling until Mary grew anxious and said, "For heavens sake, read it so I know what you are saying. Where *is* Tom? Didn't he come to California?"

"He doesn't say. Evidently not. He must have hid out for a while and then returned home just a few days after we got away. He tells here how he went to look for us and met up with the swindler that got our place. The guard must have gone to Springville and taken over the same day he got it. He showed Tom

151

our house and furniture and proposed to Tom to get rid of me if he found me."

"Why would he do that?"

"Tom was trying to find out from him what had happened to us. He probably accomplished that by pretending he was on the outs with us too. Tom says here he tried to find us at the soldiers' camp. One of the drivers told him they had seen us and we were headed for Cedar Valley."

"Why did they tell him that?"

"I don't know."

Several times during the reading of the letter they stopped to discuss it.

"Read the rest of your father's letter. Perhaps that will clear things up," John said. Mary started reading it.

The weather is very cold here at present. I did not get your letter from Boulder. William Thomas Blacklion came here to get a load of flour and said that John Rees, the blacksmith, told him that Lily your cow is with a man named Mills, near to Jordan Mill. I sent Gilam—John Atkin and Tom Roland but they did not get her and said that they did not see one that looked like her. If we get the cow we shall bring her with us. In your next letter I wish you would send the proper name and place of the man if you know it. We do not know for sure which way we shall come. If we go to San Bernadino in the Spring we shall start beginning of April, if to the north we shall start end of May, perhaps we shall stay till fall. The Welsh are all in good health. Henry Moore is recruiting soldiers and earns 30 dollars a month. J. Lewes, J. James, and Rees Davis have bought a yoke of oxen apiece. H. Moore has bought a wagon all thinking of migrating in the spring. Sneson's two sons have been buried—Martha Anne is well. Harris is in San Bernadino, C. H. Wilock lives in Harris' house. I can't read little Henry's letter very well. Send back as soon as you can telling us about the country. I hope to see your faces before long.

Daniel Thomas

"Oh, I hope we'll see them soon, too!" Mary exclaimed.

"Now you see? You had all that worry for nothing. Tom is all right and so are your parents."

They sat up most of the night discussing the news mentioned in the letters. John read Tom's letter over and over. Finally, he said, "It is a mystery where Tom was between the time I left him and the time he returned home. He doesn't say anything about going to California."

"It must have been Tom who told the soldiers to look for us along the road," Mary said.

"One thing I know is that Tom was looking for us," John said. "But it was Henry Moore that told the soldiers about us."

"But if Tom was looking for us all that time I don't see how he missed us," Mary replied.

"I do. Yet he should have known if we were getting out it was because the Avenging Angels were after us, and I would not be on the main road. It must have been later after we were with the soldiers that the driver saw me," John said.

"Then why didn't he tell Tom we were on our way to California?" Mary asked.

"That's what puzzled me at first, but you remember we were stopped when those wagons went by, and he probably didn't notice in which direction I was going was why he said I was headed for Cedar Valley."

Sometimes as they talked they would become very angry, especially the part where the guard had invited Tom in to look at their house and furniture that John had bribed him with.

"The nerve of that guard, suggesting that Tom take you out and make away with you! I wish Tom had done something to him," Mary said furiously.

"Are you suggesting Tom should have gunned him down? He was testing him out about the killings. As far as he knew that was what had happened to us. I'm sure that was their intention and he wasn't telling Tom his part in it. On the other hand, Tom was working to get all the information he could out of him. Since he was living in our house Tom knew he had some idea of what had become of us, and he wasn't about to destroy the best source of information he had. Tom knew I wouldn't have sold out to him and left the country without sending word unless we were hard put for time."

"Oh, how I hate those Polygamists!" Mary said, thinking that was the worst thing she could call them. "Do you think we will get Lily back? She was the best cow we ever had."

"I doubt very much that your father will ever see her again. I don't recall anyone by the name of Mills, but probably whoever stole the cow from us sold her to him."

"I wonder how long it will be before they get here," Mary said anxiously.

"That letter has been on the road a long time, but it will be a long time yet before the mountain passes are open for that kind of travel. Don't get your heart set on seeing them very soon," John told her.

The winter passed, spring came, and still there was no

word from the Thomases or the others coming from Utah.

In spite of the new chairs John had given Mary for Christmas and the curtains and rugs she had made out of worn-out clothing the house still did not please her. "I wish we had a better place to live before they all get here," she told John.

There was nothing he could do about it at present, so he did not reply. He was a proud man, and it hurt him that he could not provide better for his family. He worked hard every day but Sunday. In his spare time he studied diligently for the tests he would soon have to take to become an American citizen. For him that had become an obsession. He tried to persuade Mary to study also, but she always had something else to do.

Summer drew near, and John got the urge to move on, to look for farmland that he could buy. The oxen were ready to travel again. The one that had been ailing was in good shape now.

John spoke to Mary about leaving Angels Camp. She thought if they were going to move they should do it right away so they could get settled before her folks arrived.

"I will tell Mr. Shedrick to get someone to take my place as soon as he can," John said happily. He was glad that Mary was willing now to go. They could live more cheaply in the valley. The price of grain and hay was so high in the mining towns that the feed for a man's team cost almost as much as his own food.

In a few days they were ready to leave. They had accumulated so much in the short while they had lived there that they could hardly haul it all. They had a crate of chickens, a cow, a kitten, John's horse, and Rover. John said, "Looks as if we have made some gain."

They came to many crossroads, and it was hard sometimes to decide which one to take. They were beginning to see plowed fields and people more frequently. Once, after talking to a well dressed couple riding in a buggy, Mary produced a comb from somewhere and pinned her hair up. She hadn't done that since her accident. The back of her neck was healed now, but she had scars that would remain forever.

John noticed what she was doing and climbed into the wagon and sat awhile beside her. "Mary, how pretty you look today," he told her.

It was not the late evening sun that sent the warmth through her body but the tender words from John. There had been so few times during their great hardships that he had commented on her appearance.

They camped along the way and the next morning started out while it was yet dark. Since it was a cold, foggy morning the children were warmly dressed with long wool stockings and scarves and mittens, all of which Mary had knitted. She never bought anything she could make. Dawn overtook them as they came through a pass and the sun was rising directly behind them, coming up over the Sierras. With sunrise the fog and mist disappeared.

John was riding ahead on his horse, and as he came around a jut of rock a magnificent sweep of the valley came into view. Joyfully he motioned for Mary to hurry. He heard her speak to the oxen and gently touch them with the staff to coax them into a more rapid pace. The road was narrow at this point so she stopped in the middle of it. John rose up in his stirrups and pointed to the scene below.

"Hail America!" he shouted.

They gazed down on the beautiful Sacramento Valley that stretched farther than the eye could see. The grass had started to grow, and the whole valley seemed to be covered with an emerald carpet. John was spellbound at its vastness. To him it gave great promise of wealth.

"Down there lies our happiness," he said.

But Mary felt awed and frightened. Maybe it was the bigness of it—distance without end. The past year had been full of terror, and she did not feel it would be any better down there.

Without comment she started the oxen on down the road. It descended quite rapidly from there into the valley. The closer they got to Stockton the better John liked it.

"I feel now as if we wasted a lot of time up there in those mountains. We are just now seeing what I expected California to be like."

After they found a temporary place to stay in Stockton John went to see about his naturalization papers. He was to appear for the last time on April 29, 1859, at the courthouse in Stockton, San Joaquin County. He was a proud man when he returned with his application. It stated his intention of becoming a citizen of the United States of America. He made the children stand quietly beside their mother while he read it to them. He raised his voice a bit higher when he came to the part where he "renounced forever all allegiance and fidelity to any foreign Prince, Potentate, State or Sovereignty whatever and particularly to the Queen of Great Britain" of whom he had hitherto been a subject.

John went every day on his horse to look for land. A house did not matter to him; he could build one after he got crops planted. Fertile soil with plenty of water—that was what he was looking for. He found places he liked but he did not have enough money to buy, and he was determined not to settle for anything less than he wanted, so he kept looking until it was too late in the season for planting.

Mary became impatient because she wanted to be settled before her folks arrived. It seemed to John that there was always something pushing him, so when a Mr. Leach near Lockford offered him a nice house in return for hauling, he took it in order to satisfy Mary. They moved into the Charles Leach house on May 29, 1859. John did other hauling, too, when not working for Mr. Leach. Sometimes he worked for money; sometimes in exchange for hay and other produce.

Mary was delighted with the house. It was large enough to accommodate the other members of the Thomas family, too, if they ever arrived. Mary was afraid they might have left before her last instructions reached them. If so, they might never find each other again. But at last the letter arrived.

Camp Floyd June 10, 1859

Dear Children John and Mary Griffiths,

Once again I am taking the opportunity of writing to you hoping that you are well as we are at present. Received your letter dated April informing us that you were well. We have been here two weeks waiting for the floods to pass by, the rivers are still very high. We are thinking of starting tomorrow and coming the north road in company with Henry Moore—John Lewes—John James—Stephen Lilly and two other wagons.

Two company of soldiers will come with us as an escort, one company of cavalry. I wish you would send me a letter to Carson Valley. I will send letters again if I have the opportunity. We will start with 2 wagons, 29 head of cattle, 2 mares, 2 colts, 1 pony—10 of the above are milk cows and six heifers a year old.

If successful we shall be in Carson in 6 or 7 weeks.

"Father was in such a hurry he did not even sign his name. He said they might start the next day. They could be here tomorrow!" Mary said.

"Maybe not tomorrow, but they should be here soon. It is too late to get a letter to them at Carson now," John replied.

CHAPTER TWENTY-NINE

Little May, who was now past two years old, was playing on her swing, which was tied to a branch of the big oak tree that shaded the house. She was watching a cloud of dust in the distance. As it came nearer she could see the long procession of wagons and riders and cattle and horses and people. It was not an unfamiliar sight, and she was about to turn away when they stopped and opened the gate to the road leading up to the house.

"Mamma, Mamma!" May called.

When Mary opened the door the party was close enough that she could hear the wagons and the lowing of the cattle. She could see her father standing by the gate, so she ran down the hill. When he saw her coming he ran to meet her.

"I knew it, I knew it. I had a feeling you would come today!" Mary said, clasped in her father's arms.

Tom saw Mary running down the hill, and he rode up from the rear where he had been helping to keep the stock in check. Mary simply went to pieces when she saw him.

"We thought you were dead," she kept saying.

"I'm anything but dead!" Tom said boisterously, and he swept her up off her feet and began to swing her round and round. Mary screamed and nearly fainted in his arms. Months had passed since her back had been burned, but still it was so tender that any hard pressure was extremely painful.

"What is the matter? What have I done?" he asked, gently letting her down.

They all felt great pity when Mary lifted up the back of her blouse and showed them her scars. The new flesh was so thin there were little droplets of blood seeping out of some of the deeply burned scars from Tom's rough embrace.

John and Johnny came from the fields, and there was more rejoicing. They talked until the stock began to mill around and get out of hand. There was not just Mr. Thomas's stock; the others had brought cattle and horses, too. John opened the gate to the corral he had ready for this occasion. He was glad he had accommodations for them, and he was as proud as Mary of the house.

"John, do you recognize some of those cows as your own? I managed to get hold of the young stock you left in the far field. I kept the heifers. They made good cows, and I brought them to you. The others I sold for you for a good price," Mr. Thomas said.

John expressed his gratitude.

There was so much news to catch up on that Mary, Sally, Letticia, and the other women were all talking at once. There were a great many children. Sally had a little boy named Willie, six months old, that Mary didn't know about. John and Tom made an excuse to go look at the stock in order to talk without interruption. They had many things to explain to each other.

"What ever happened to you the night I left you headed for California?" John demanded immediately.

"I started out, but the farther I got the more cowardly I felt—like I was running out on you and sis," he said.

"Where did you go then?" John asked.

"I was just about to turn back when I overtook a man alone. He was going to Copper Mountain with a string of burros to get out some ore. Said he had hoped to hire some men, but everyone had been pressed into army service, coerced by the Mormons, or attracted by the pay from the United States government. It struck me that it might be a good chance to hide for a while, so I hired out to him and never left the place. But I was so worried about you and sis I finally quit and went home. I wrote to you how I found things."

They talked about it for a long time. Many things had happened in Salt Lake City that were never explained. They decided it was best to forget—as the Mormons did.

Later on the men asked John about the country and the possibilities of making a living. He told them he was still looking for land and was starting out the next morning to investigate a rumor he had heard. "The state is opening up some farmland we can get possession of by some kind of land grant. It is an inducement to get farmers to settle here in California."

All were interested except Henry Moore. "I think I will look for a job," he said. "I'd rather live here awhile before I invest in land."

"If you want work I heard they need men over at the coal mine," John told him.

"Where is that?" Henry asked.

"It's in the mountains between here and the coast, south of Antioch."

"How far?"

"I don't know exactly, but not over fifty miles. You could be pretty sure of a job, I can tell you that. Some people call it the Welshman's show because it's operated by a group of coal miners from Wales, and I hear they give preference to their own nationality."

The next morning the Moores took off for the coal mines. The women were disappointed. They had hoped they'd all be neighbors.

John and the other men left for Stockton about the same time.

Tom had decided to set up a blacksmith shop and spotted the ideal location on the way. He liked the four corners at the crossroads at Waterloo. Eventually he found the owner and was able to make a deal.

The other men continued on toward Stockton. They inquired at the courthouse and found that forty-acre parcels could be had for a small purchase price if they agreed to farm the land and to build a house on it in a given length of time. The new state of California was anxious to attract farmers from the east.

"Would forty acres be sufficient?" some of the men asked.

John explained that root crops could be raised there most all year, and for those who wanted to have sheep or cattle, there was plenty of free range.

Mr. Thomas, Mr. Lewes, Mr. Lilly, and John kept looking at the land described in the government notice. Lewes and Lilly found places to their liking, but John and Mr. Thomas kept holding out for a place with a stream running through it.

They finally heard of another tract of government land and went to look at it. There were two plots side by side, far better than any they had seen. There was no creek, but they decided to take it regardless. It took in the top of a knoll and ran down the east side to the valley. The grass in the valley was three feet high. From the top of the knoll the panoramic view extended for miles. Looking down over the valley they could see a small schoolhouse not far away. Other farms were scattered here and there, several miles apart. It was a beautiful location.

"I don't know about you, John, but I am ready to stop looking," Mr. Thomas said.

"I am of the same opinion. I haven't see anything better than this," John replied.

They rode toward some tall palm trees, and got off their horses to view the place more closely. It looked as if there had once been a building there that had burned down. The fire had killed most of the trees.

"There must have been an old Spanish house here," John said.

They looked up the cornerstones and marked them on their map so they would apply for the right piece of ground. They were happy with their find and hurried home to tell about it.

Mary and Sally were anxious to be neighbors, so the men knew their decision to take this piece of ground would please them. They planned to go to Stockton the next day and make application for it.

When they arrived home they both described the land in an identical way. "I know you will like it. It is a beautiful location on top of a rolling hill where there was once an old Spanish house with palm trees around it," they said.

The two men had failed to discuss which piece of ground each would take. So it was a surprise to John when Sally came rushing in to say, "Mary, it's unbelievable, but your pa is going to build me a house in a palm grove. I can hardly wait to see the place!"

As she left the room, John said, "Well, that settles that."

"Settles what?" Mary asked.

"Which piece of ground you and I will own."

"Does it make a difference?" Mary asked.

"Well, not really. But I was of the opinion it hadn't been decided yet."

On their way into Stockton next day Mr. Thomas said: "Now, John, you file on whichever plot you want. You found it, so you take first choice." John felt better that Mr. Thomas had given him a choice, but naturally he took the one without the palm grove.

CHAPTER THIRTY

The Thomases and the Griffiths moved as soon as the papers were approved. They lived in the wagons while buildings were put up and fences constructed.

John built his house by an old oak tree, half of which was gone. It looked as if it had been struck by lightning. But half a tree was better than none; it afforded some shade and a limb on which to put a swing for the children. Mr. Thomas and John helped each other when there were heavy timbers to be put up. When Mr. Thomas cleared out to build his house he found it necessary to uproot all but one of the palm trees. They were so nearly dead that it wasn't safe to leave them standing.

It was cheaper to buy small logs to build with than to buy lumber. Both houses were built with the main house as living quarters and bedrooms on each end. The lean-to on the back served as wood-shed, kitchen, and storeroom. The houses had dirt floors which were packed so hard they could be swept clean.

One day John and Mr. Thomas drove into Stockton for supplies. While John loaded the wagon Mr. Thomas said, "I'll go see if there are any letters."

When he returned he had a letter in his hand. "It's for you, John."

John reached for it and saw to his joy that it was from his brother David. He'd given up ever hearing from his family. He wanted to tear it open and read it as fast as he could, yet something held him back. He felt he wanted to be alone when he read it. So he put it unopened in his shirt pocket.

John could think of nothing else all the way home, but not until he had unhitched the team and hung the harness up did he sit down and carefully break the seal. He noticed by the date that the letter was over a year old.

As John read the letter he stopped often to wipe tears from his eyes. There in the stillness of the barn he felt so far away from all his people. It took him a long time to read the letter, and when he had finished he turned the pages over and read them again—this time more slowly. Nothing that he read or thought could stamp out the picture of his brother James lying in a coffin with his baby on his arm. John had often thought that he might never see his mother or father again... "But not Jim!" he said aloud.

John got only halfway to the house when he met Mary coming to look for him. She knew the minute she looked at him that something was wrong.

"What is the matter, John?" she asked, taking hold of his arm.

"I received a letter from home. My brother James is dead."

"Oh, I'm sorry, John."

They walked on into the house, and after John put the packages onto the table he started to hand the letter to her, then drew it back again and held it for a moment before he gave it to her.

"John, if you don't want me to read it, I understand."

"No, it is not that I don't want you to read it, but it will make you cry," he said.

Mary did cry. She wanted to relieve John's sorrow somehow, but she could think of nothing more than to be near him and to listen when the time came that he wanted to talk about it.

John and Mr. Thomas labored many hours to make their farms productive. It was necessary to sink deep wells for water. Everything they did took a lot of time and money. Mr. Thomas started right in raising sheep and did well. He was able to get grazing land close by, which left all of his good land for raising hay and grain. Benjamin was old enough now to help, and everything seemed to go well for them.

John wanted no part of raising sheep. He started in again with cattle, but the land was too dry to support cattle, and he was forced to buy hay for them. Mr. Thomas tried to get him to switch to sheep, but he said he could not stand their smell and bleating. Then he started looking for other land.

John had seen farms along the San Joaquin River with good all-year pastures. He traveled south along the river until he came to its confluence with the Stanislaus River. Each year they overflowed their banks and enriched the soil in the meadows. John walked through fields of wild grass that was knee high in places. The cattle were fat and stood chewing their cuds in the shade of the willows. It was the kind of place he had dreamed of. He could see a great future for them here.

John hunted up the owner and found it could be purchased for far less than he had expected. He bought it without even considering what Mary or her father might say.

"We are settled here, John; the children are content; the land is paid for, and our houses are built. We might not do so well here, son, but where a tether fastens, a horse must browse," his father-in-law said.

Mary flatly refused to go.

"We will never be prosperous here," John argued.

"But we have all we need, and we are happy God has supplied us. Why can't you dig ditches here as you did in Utah?" she asked.

"I could dig ditches, Mary, but pray tell me, where is the water to come from? I can't believe God will supply that. There are some things we have to supply for ourselves," John said.

"I will not fix up another house and then leave it." Mary turned and left the room, which meant she was through arguing about it.

John was just as determined, so he went alone. He removed most of the stock to the new ranch and worked both places.

In October, 1860, Mary gave birth to another daughter. She was named Fanny after John's youngest sister.

It was lonely and hard for everyone with John living one place and Mary another, so Mary finally gave in and moved to the river ranch.

CHAPTER THIRTY-ONE

As they circled down to the river the green fields seemed even more vast than when John had been there before. The water in the rivers had receded, so there was more land showing.

"The grass is almost as green here as it is in Wales!" Mary exclaimed.

Already the sandy loam was of the right firmness to plow, and John was eager to get started. Since everyone had opposed him in this venture he felt he had to succeed. The willows and the cottonwoods along the riverbanks were starting to put on their bright summer green. A sweet, earthy smell arose from the sun-warmed ground. John was more pleased with his land every time he looked at it. They all went down to the river's edge and felt of the running water. Mary thought the place was even more beautiful than he had described it.

"Just think, this is all ours—the land, the planted fields, and all of the ground next to the river is black loam," he said.

"I'll admit it is better looking farmland than we had at Lockford. I can understand now why you were so anxious to move here. But happiness is more important than riches."

"I will not contradict that, but in this case I don't see why we can't have both," John replied.

He told Johnny to round up the cattle and see if any were missing. He wasn't really worried about the cattle, but he knew Johnny hated farm work and that would be something he would enjoy doing. John wanted his son to be satisfied there so that when he grew up he would not want to leave farming for some other occupation.

When he brought the cattle in, with Rover's help, they were so fat from having all the feed they could eat John hardly recognized his own stock.

"You see, Mary, the cattle are almost in shape to take to the market just from grazing on the wild grass. I can't see how we can lose here," he said with confidence.

The yield from the rich loam was tremendous. Once again Mary had bins of golden grain to sift through her fingers. But they still did not have a decent house to live in. The farm was all meadows and floodland. There was not a building site on the whole 354 acres that was not threatened once each year by overflowing rivers.

Years passed, and they continued to live in the unpainted shack that John erected when he first moved there. Barns and sheds and fences had to be built first to keep up with the increasing crops and stock. There was never time to build the house that he kept promising.

It did not help that the family kept increasing. Not long after they moved back to the ranch a second son was born. He was named after Mary's brother Tom. John was proud that he had another son.

He had applied for citizenship and knew that someday he would be called in to take the examination. Each night, thereafter, regardless of how tired he was, he would get out his books and study. He was eager to become a citizen of the United States, and he did not want to fail. It took a great deal of time to learn all the history of the country and the functions of the United States government.

Finally a letter came telling John to appear in Stockton, April 13, 1864, to take his final examination for citizenship. John had impressed upon his family what an important occasion this was. He had made application five years earlier and had studied every one of the books recommended to him—and more. He could repeat all of the Declaration of Independence and knew most of the Constitution by heart. He knew how the government functioned and some of the laws of the states. California was so new there was not much he could learn about it from books.

He was confident when he entered the courthouse, and smiling when he came out. He passed the tests easily and from that date on had every right of a freeborn American. He was always interested in public affairs and would ride a great distance to take part in a community meeting of government, school, or church.

In the spring of 1864 another child was born. Mary no longer had time to help with the chores. John had hoped for another boy, since he would need lots of help in the future if his plans for expansion were to be carried out. The baby was a curly-haired little girl. Two years later another boy was born, and soon following him was another girl. The house was overflowing. Two large barns had been built, and sheds were full of machinery. There were fences and corrals, sties and poultry houses. Soon a new home would be in the making.

Even though they were doing well enough, the last two years had been mediocre. Several times they had been forced by the high water to move out and take the stock to higher ground until the river receded. It was hard on them, and always there were some losses. Floors in the buildings would be covered with a foot or so of silt, mud, and sand. Fences would be washed away. And the well would be contaminated so that all water had to be boiled. First one would be sick and then another.

Flies and mosquitoes multiplied during those damp years. Mary always kept camphor in the house and smudge pots burning outside the doors; still the insects got in to disturb their sleep, and the children had great welts on their bodies from the bites. Even in the face of financial success, they had worries.

May developed a cough, and then Fanny. John could see for himself that they would have to move to higher ground. He would not sacrifice the health of his family to gain wealth. He could see how fragile Fanny was, and with this in mind he told Mary he was moving her and the children back to live beside her father and Sally.

Mary protested that John couldn't stay there alone—he did not look well, either. But at the time there didn't seem to be any other solution.

"School will soon be out, and Johnny will be here to help me," he said. Johnny was attending a boarding school in Stockton.

Mary was torn between her duties. The doctor said Fanny must be moved to where the air and ground were not so damp. Her cough had grown worse, and she was pale and listless. She hardly ever ran and played with the other children any more.

If there was a favorite child in the family, it was Fanny. Just when Mary would decide she could not leave John, Fanny would go into a fit of coughing. One morning after Fanny had had an extremely hard time John told Mary to start packing and to take everything except what he would need to batch with. The big wagon was loaded to the brim, and they started for Lockford the next morning.

It was the first time Charley and the baby, Rose, had been off the place. John was driving a fine span of horses now. Only the two youngest children and Fanny rode in the wagon.

May, Tommy, and Peggy all had riding horses.

In a way Mary hated to move back to the old place as much as she had hated to move away from it. They had done so well in the new location. In a few more years they would have all the money they would ever need and would not have to put so much back into the place. They had enough cows now, and their herd was increasing fast. They had lots of horses, too. It seemed as if Johnny was always breaking a new pony. Sometimes Mary wondered how she had managed on the meager existence they had had before moving to the river ranch.

Sally and Mr. Thomas could hardly believe it when they looked across to John and Mary's old house and saw them getting out of the wagon. It made their hearts ache when they saw little Fanny so ill. John had to carry her into the house.

"Whatever have you done to my poor baby?" Sally asked, as tears sprang to her eyes. Although Sally had a large family, she always had room in her heart for Mary's children and worried as much over them as she did over her own.

John stayed only long enough to get them settled. With a heavy heart he left the next morning before the children awoke. He felt he could not tell Fanny good-bye. He hoped and prayed this move would hasten her recovery.

When he kissed Mary good-bye and told her to take good care of the children, she clung to him saying, "I have done everything I know to do, but I am afraid our little Fanny will not live."

"You must have faith. You know the Lord is our divine healer, and he will see us through."

For some time after the children awoke and found that their father had already gone, the room was filled with the sound of their sobbing.

As the months passed by, May grew stronger but Fanny continued about the same—sometimes able to go outside and play with the other children, then for no apparent reason slipping back again. After each attack it would take a little longer for her to regain her strength.

Their house was built on the crest of a hill with a panoramic view of the valley and of the one-room schoohouse not over a mile away. Fanny would sit in the window at home and watch Tommy and Peggy and Sally's children, Willie and Martha, as they came home from school. It was quicker for them to cut across the fields than to follow the road.

It made Mary's heart ache when Fanny asked over and over, "Please, Mama, can't I go to school tomorrow?"

"Not tomorrow, dear, but someday soon I hope," her mother would reply, knowing that she would probably never be able to go.

Mary had May at home as well as Fanny. May had finished all the grades taught at the little valley school and was eager to go away to boarding school like Johnny and Sally's older children. Mary would tell her, "Next year, when you are sixteen, you may go. In the meantime study from the books Johnny brought you."

Mary received a letter from Johnny saying he was sick with the measles. That added to her worries. He recovered in time to come home for the holiday vacation, however, and Mary sent him right on to the San Joaquin to help his father. He went reluctantly because he still hated farming, but he went because his mother asked him to.

They were all together for Christmas, and Mary often looked upon it as their happiest one. Fanny seemed much better, and May was practically well. For once, there was money to spend for things other than necessities. The children put their savings together and bought Fanny a little blue flowered tea set.

Spring came early. There was very little rain in February, and John left earlier than usual for the other ranch. The winter had been hard on Fanny, and Mary was anxious for summer to come.

Then one evening Mary and Tommy were at the barn milking when Peggy came running out to the barn screaming, "Mamma, Mamma, May said to come quick! Something is the matter with Fanny!"

CHAPTER THIRTY-TWO

Mary found May holding Fanny's forehead with one hand while with the other hand she held a pan into which Fanny was vomiting.

As soon as they could get her quieted, Mary put her to bed and sent Peggy to tell her grandfather to go as fast as he could for a doctor. Sally came right over, but it was hours before the doctor arrived. After he examined her he said he thought it was something she had eaten that did not agree with her, then added that there was a lot of sickness this time of year in the valley. He left some medicine and advised Mary to keep her in bed and feed her only soup and liquids for a few days. He said he believed that she would be all right, but Mary knew better. Early the following morning she started Tommy out for the San Joaquin ranch to tell John. He was a little boy to send so far alone, but there was no one else to go.

"It is a long way," she told him. "Don't run the horse too fast...just keep going at a steady gait. Don't get off your horse any more than you have to—and don't take any shortcuts; stay on the main road. Tell your father to come at once."

Every time Tommy would start, she would call out something else for him to look out for.

"Mind you fill your canteen...and take some oats for the horse."

"I will Mamma."

She kissed him good-bye, then hurried back to sit beside Fanny. Her fingers were never idle, and as she sat she twisted fibers into threads at her spinning wheel. The hours of the day passed quickly, but the night seemed long. Fanny awoke intermittently and would always ask in her faint little voice, "Are you there, Mamma?"

"Yes, dear, Mamma is always here!"

Finally it was daylight, and Sally came and insisted that Mary lie down for a while. She was so exhausted that she did fall asleep but slept for only a short time. Besides being worried over Fanny, who had steadily grown worse, she was also concerned about Tommy and began to imagine all sorts of terrible things had happened to him.

Sally could see that Fanny was much worse. Several times while she sat there she leaned closer to be sure the child was still breathing. She sent for Mr. Thomas, and when he came she told him he must prepare Mary, for the end was near.

When John arrived he found everything in a state of confusion. On entering the house he met May weeping and wringing her hands. He soon reached the bedroom where Mary was on her knees beside Fanny's bed. She had knelt in that position for hours, caressing Fanny's feverish brow and kissing her thin little hands, beseeching God not to take her away. Mary felt she could not accept so great a blow.

By sheer force John drew her out of the room. One look at little Fanny, and he knew he had come too late. He enfolded Mary in his arms when he saw Sally come out of the room and softly close the door.

"The Lord giveth, and the Lord taketh away," she said.

At those words John could not restrain a long and bitter groan. Little Fanny Griffiths was buried April 12, 1872, in the Harmony Grove Cemetery near Stockton. A little white lamb was placed on her tombstone.

For Christmas Johnny had made a small wooden chest for Fanny to keep her belongings in. Now May gathered up Fanny's favorite possessions and some of her clothes and packed them into the chest. Once when Fanny had been feverish her mother had cut her braids off so her hair could be more easily combed. May put the braids and some flowers from her grave and the little tea set into the chest, too. All the children came with something of Fanny's to put in; then the chest was nailed shut.

It promised to be a good year for the farmers. The weather had been mild and the crops were coming on early. John ambled through the fields to see how they had grown while he was away. Not having any family at the ranch now, he spent very little time at the house. He threw himself into his work so there would be no time for reflection.

He felt partly to blame for the long suffering and death of Fanny because of the conditions they had lived under at the ranch. He should never have moved his family there in the first place, he thought.

During the time John was clearing new land by grubbing out the willows he hauled the trees and the debris washed down by the river each year to a piece of ground above the old house. Here he piled them up in order to make a building site above the flood waters. After a few years it began to look like a dam. John could picture what a big house would look like built up there. It would be seen from afar and would be dry and safe for the family.

Nearly all of the place was planted in crops this year, so most of the stock was turned out to graze on government land. During the plowing and planting season John had hired some extra hands to help. He looked forward to the time when his three sons could assist him. John was a proud man and he had decided from now on there would be no more manual labor by Mary or the girls. He expected to make enough from this year's crops to build the new house and have money left over.

Johnny was taking a course in architecture and building at school in Stockton, and he had brought home blueprints of houses he had drawn. Mary picked out the one she liked best. That was the one John planned to build.

Although John was terribly overworked, he let the extra hands go as soon as the crops were in. During the growing period there would be a lull. By harvesttime both Johnny and Tommy would be able to help, and perhaps now that there were no more children on the way or sickness among them Mary would consent to come during the harvest and cook for them.

John knew where he could get a scoop shovel. He hitched four horses to it and filled in and leveled off the building site. It was looking good, and he could hardly wait for Mary to see it. It was to be more or less a surprise.

The plan Mary had chosen was a two-story house with an upper porch. John dreamed about how on a summer evening they could sit out on the porch and view the entire ranch. He became exuberant with the thought that at last success was nearly in his grasp. He had almost reached the goal he had set for himself when he came to America. By becoming a citizen of the United States he felt he had gained full freedom from the hands of any governing powers, and now prosperity was just around the corner.

John spent the next few days checking on his cattle and horses that were out on open range. He found most of them feeding along the river bottom. He decided to cut the hay early this year so he could get the stock back into his own pasture. If he had them fenced in he would not have to ride so far to check on them.

Before John arrived home it began to rain. The showers continued all night and the next day. John did only the chores that were necessary. He stayed inside and made a mental estimate of what this year's income would be. Everyone said there would be bumper crops because weather conditions had been perfect.

It was a warm rain, and John knew if it kept up it would melt the snow in the mountains. He began to wonder if there was going to be a flood. If so, he had better start putting things that would be ruined by water up in the lofts of the barns and rafters of the house. He thought of the young calves in a pasture across the river and decided to go bring them in. It didn't take much rain to raise it above the fording level.

Coming back he had a hard time getting them safely across, not only because of the high water but because he was not able to make the dog go where he told him. He hadn't had a good dog on the place since Rover died. The children played with the dogs so much he could not train them well.

John went twice in the night with his lantern to check the water level in the Stanislaus, since it was the nearest to the house. Now the rain came in flurries accompanied by great bursts of wind. John could hear loose objects blowing around outside. Then the storm let up, and the moon shone through. John thought it was over and fell asleep.

He was awakened in the early hours to find rain coming down harder than ever. At daybreak he went again to look at the water levels, but he did not go far. It was already up to the buildings! He waded through great pools to get to the barn. He had never seen rivers rise so quickly. A few more hours of this and water would be all over the place.

He took the farm horses from the barn, opened the outside gate, and chased them through it to find higher ground for themselves. Many of his cattle and horses that had been feeding along the river had now come home and were milling outside the gate.

It was here on John's place that the flood waters of the two rivers met and made currents which dredged out deep holes and washed away the land. As yet this storm had done little damage to his crops, but what worried him was the rising temperature. Melted snow along with the rain meant that by tomorrow he would have water over most of his fields. All he could do was pray it would quit raining.

But the rain continued all week, with the water getting nearer to the house. He had turned the chickens out and they were gathered on the high ground that he had built up for the new house. When he saw them there he thought of the time he'd lost an entire crop to the grasshoppers in Utah. He felt he could not face another setback such as that and grew almost hysterical when he realized it was possible that disaster would strike again.

He was so determined there would be no destruction that he put up props and even tried to build a barricade to turn the water away from the buildings. He could not accomplish much by himself. If he had been thinking more rationally he would have known he was only using his strength unnecessarily. Nothing he could do would stop it: he was one man against two raging rivers. He watched as the big gate that opened to the barn lot was washed loose. Desperately he ran out into the water and tied a rope to it, then with all his strength pulled and tugged to get it turned to where he could secure it to a two-by-four by the barn door. He was near collapse when he noticed water seeping into the house. He knew now that the snow had melted. Never had he seen the water come up as fast as it was now, and the crest was nowhere near. He knew the only thing he could do now was to save himself. The flood was coming at him like some monster trying to destroy him, and all his work and prayers could not stop it.

"Where is God?" he cried out, and the tears mixed with the rain and ran down his face. He was so exhausted he could no longer control his emotions. "Will these catastrophes never end?" he cried.

He ran to the outside gate, glad that the horses had stayed there. He started to lead two horses back, then decided he had best put two teams on. There was so much already piled in the wagon, small tools and saddles and blankets from the barn, that one team would never pull it. The road would be soggy and the ground so full of water it would hardly hold the weight of a man. He was sinking down almost to his shoe tops, which made it hard to get the horses hitched and the wagon ready to go.

When he was ready to leave, John kept delaying, praying for the rain to stop. If it stopped now he might not lose all of the crop. He tied his riding horse to the back of the wagon so if he had to abandon it he could get out on horseback. This was the highest water he had ever seen.

While John was checking the harness to see that everything was fastened he heard a rider coming at a full gallop. "For God's sake, get out as fast you can!" he shouted. A dam has broken above Knights Ferry!" And he rode away to warn others as quickly as he had come.

John knew that was it. He'd have to run, leaving his land and dreams behind.

CHAPTER THIRTY-THREE

Mary was terribly worried. There was flooding all over the country, and she knew that John was in trouble. She heard reports of farms near theirs being under water, so knew their place would be—yet John did not come. She made up her mind if he did not arrive by the next day she would go to see where he was.

Early the next morning she saw him coming. She put on her coat and scarf and ran out to open the gate, but he got there first. When he got down from the wagon he was so exhausted he reeled and nearly fell down.

"Are you sick...or hurt?" Mary asked, running to take hold of his arm.

"Neither. I am just worn out, and I can't remember when I last ate anything," he said.

"You go on to the house and send Tommy to help me unhitch. We will put the horses in the barn," Mary told him.

John staggered into the house, his legs stiff from sitting so long in the wet wagon.

While Mary prepared breakfast John told her about the flood and the dam breaking.

"Do you think it will wash the buildings away?" she asked.

"Some were already gone, but the house will stand...and the barns. I built them well, but I am afraid the crops will be gone. We might still get one cutting of hay if the water goes down soon," he said.

But the rain continued several more days. Then the sun came out, and as soon as John was sure the water had gone down he went back to the ranch. He knew his loss would be great, but he was not prepared for what he saw.

Not one building was left. The site he had prepared for the new house had acted like a wing dam, forcing the full impact of the water from the broken dam against the barns. In the place where he had scooped out gravel from the riverbank it looked as if there had been a great whirlpool. Boulders covered the spot where the yard had been. The water had taken not only the crops but acres of topsoil. The river had changed its course so that now one pasture was the new channel.

John was a defeated man. As he remembered where things had been he went to look for them. It seemed that as much

175

debris had washed in as had washed away. He stopped to examine a section of roof and discovered it had been painted—it wasn't even his! The flood was widespread, and he was not the only one who was hurt. It gave him a certain amount of solace to know that others had been flooded out where they had tried to make homes.

There seemed to be very little he could salvage. The only thing standing was the wreckage of the old house. John got on his horse and rode away from where the buildings had been, trying to gain the will to start over again.

After a few days of digging out fence rows and gathering pieces of this and that out of the stinking mud, John lost the will to go on. Without even rounding up the cattle and horses which he hoped were somewhere in the vicinity, he went home.

Mary heard there was a place in town set up to aid the flood victims. Many who had been washed out had no place to go. When she told John about it and suggested that they might ask for help, he became extremely angry. "I don't need aid from anyone!" he said resentfully.

"They are helping all those who were washed out. We can get free seed, to replant the crops."

"Isn't it enough to have had to suffer being flooded out without being humiliated too? I don't need charity; you don't need charity; our children don't need charity. And you can also tell your father that I don't want his sheep."

"All right, I will tell Father," Mary snapped back at him. She was disgusted but knew there was no use arguing.

On Sunday they all attended the service of the Reorganized Church of the Latter Day Saints. It was a most interesting meeting for John, as it had to do with Salt Lake City.

The presiding elder read the following proclamation:

> We, The Reorganized Church of Jesus Christ of Latter Day Saints, proclaim the church in Utah has materially and largely departed from the faith and doctrines, law and ordinances of the original church of the Latter Day Saints and has corporated into its system of faith the doctrines of celestial marriage and a plurality of wives contrary to the laws and constitution of the original church.

With a vote from the congregation the elder renounced the Salt Lake church and went on to say: "In order to enable us to better carry on the work of building up the kingdom of God, and to redeem the scattered Saints from false guidance from the above-mentioned church in Utah, I appeal to all Saints whom the Lord hath made stewards through the bishop of the Reorganized Church. We need missionaries to go to England, Scotland, and Wales to work there to undo the wrong that has been done to the people by the other church."

John made up his mind quickly. He cast his lot with the group and became active in its cause. He wished he were free to go on a mission, as there was no one who knew more about what went on in the Salt Lake church than he. On the way home he told Mary of his desire to go to Wales.

"The sermon today really hit me hard. I was one of those men the elder spoke about who influenced others to join the Mormons. Little did I realize then what was to happen later in Salt Lake City."

"The gospel you believed in then is the same today. It was Brigham Young who changed," Mary replied.

"How true that is, and it all seems so incredible. At one time I considered Brigham my best friend." There was a sadness in his voice that indicated he still regretted the way things had turned out between them. There was no way they could ever be friends again.

There were other farmers at the church meeting who had suffered losses because of the flood. Most all had accepted it as an act of God and were making the best of it. Talking to these other people gave John hope, but he needed money too. He could do nothing without equipment, and it would take a lot of money for seed to plant a farm the size of his. He was determined to go at it in a big way and not start at the bottom again. Also he was not going to ask for county aid as Mary wanted him to do. To him it was still charity.

"We are not poverty stricken," he told her.

"Where is the seed to come from, then?" she asked.

"There is a man who wants to buy this place," he told her for the first time.

"You wouldn't sell this place, would you, John?" she asked.

"I have already given him my answer. He wants it for pasture only, and we can live here as long as we wish. By then I will have the house you have always wanted built at the river ranch."

Mary stood wringing her hands, knowing she could not stop him now no matter what she said.

"Don't you worry about it, Mary," John said. "You won't have to make any changes for a long time."

As soon as he got the money for the place he bought the seed and equipment he could not get along without and went back to San Joaquin to start all over again.

Mary offered to go with him, but he refused. There was no place for her at the ranch.

John was surprised how much better the place looked now than when he had last seen it after the flood. The trees were leafed out, the wild grass was growing, and the rivers were flowing serenely again. Filled with hope, he set to work in earnest.

Every day he watched for his sons. He had left word for them to come as soon as Johnny finished his term of school in Stockton. When they did not show up after a few weeks, John made the trip back to Lockford to see what had happened.

"Johnny is getting out of hand," his mother said.

"In what way?" John asked.

"He came home on Saturday after school was out and left the next morning. I tried to make him take Tommy and go and help you as you told me to, but he was determined to go back to town," Mary said.

At first John was furious. He'd been counting on the boys' help. If Johnny had been there he would no doubt have received some sort of punishment.

"I wanted to go and help you, Papa," Tommy said.

"Get ready then, because we will start back tomorrow. I will return by way of Stockton and pick up Johnny. He needs to learn where his bread and butter come from."

Mary was nearly always against punishing the children, but when Johnny refused to help his father in order to stay in town, she would not intervene. She was worried over her husband's health. He was working too hard at the ranch.

When they got inside, Mary gave John a letter Johnny had left for him. After John read it he said to Mary: "This work Johnny is doing this summer is part of his schooling, his apprenticeship. Didn't you read this letter?"

"What does that mean?" Mary asked.

"It means he is learning his trade by practical experience working under a skilled instructor. He will get credits for it at the school as well as some pay," John explained. "Didn't he tell you that?"

"No, he said he had accepted a job in town and had to be sure to be there Monday morning. He also said he hoped never to do ranch work again." Mary spoke in a tone that showed her disapproval of Johnny's behavior.

John finished reading Johnny's note before he said any more. The note explained that he had been selected for this summer job because of his excellent grades at Pacific College where he was studying to be a draftsman. He would be working under a contractor and builder where he could make use of his education. He hoped his parents would understand.

John handed the note to Mary. "Read this over again and you will understand why Johnny isn't coming to work on the ranch. Our son has become a man."

"You will be going to Stockton after him, won't you?" Mary asked.

"I will be going to Stockton, but only to give Johnny my blessing," he said.

It was a bitter disappointment to John because he had looked forward to the time when Johnny was grown and they could operate the ranch together. He went back to it now with only half the enthusiasm he had had before. Tommy was company, but too young to be of much help.

One day John looked up from his work and saw three riders coming. "I think we are about to have some company," he said to Tommy.

"Are you Mr. Griffiths?" one of the well-dressed men who had just ridden up asked.

"I am," John replied.

"Then you are the man we are looking for. We were here a few days ago," he said.

"I have another place at Lockford where I live," John explained.

"Looks like the flood washed you out," the man said, looking around at the lumber and pieces of equipment John had dug out and was cleaning up.

"Not completely," John replied. He wondered what they wanted.

"We heard you lost all your buildings. That's too bad," the man said.

"It will not happen again. I have learned not to build so close to the river." John made his answers short.

"There is a lot of work to be done here. Would you consider selling?"

"What made you think this place is for sale? Most of my land here is not hurt at all. Back where there was only high water even the fences are intact." John was indignant. He was sure they were figuring he was down and out and they could buy his place for nothing.

"I am not trying to belittle your propery, Mr. Griffiths," he said.

"On the contrary," one of the other men said, "we recognized this as being one of the best sections of land along the river. We hope to obtain three sections in this vicinity. There is a man of means in San Francisco backing us, and we are prepared to give you a substantial price for it."

"I might consider selling if the price is right," John answered.

"What would you call a fair price?" the first speaker asked.

"Since you approached me with the deal, you make the offer," John replied, still thinking no matter what it was he would turn it down.

"All right, sir, would you consider thirty dollars per acre a fair price?"

John was stunned. That was three times what he had paid for it and twice as much as he expected they would offer. But he didn't want to make a hasty decision.

"I'll have to think it over," he said.

"Of course. Can we contact you here tomorrow?"

"Yes—I can decide by then," John answered.

CHAPTER THIRTY-FOUR

This was a hard decision for John. He had made plans and had returned to carry them out. If he had two or three years without a flood he would be able to put up better buildings than he had before, and if they were built away from the river on concrete foundations they would be safe. Then he could move his family here again. Tommy and Charley would be able to help in a few years—but then he remembered how he'd counted on Johnny. He knew he could not expect his sons to want to be farmers.

He calculated on a piece of paper how much he would have if he sold out. It was almost a fortune! With it he could return to Wales. He would have money to spend. He would be able to offer his services to the church.

He did not sleep all night, weighing one answer against the other. He wanted so much to make a trip to Wales to see his family that he decided to sell. After all, he could get another place whenever he wanted to, but he might never have that much money at one time again.

The men were back the next day at the scheduled time, and John told them he was willing to sell.

"I will need a little time to round up my stock," he said.

"Take all the time you need," they replied.

John agreed to meet them the next day in Stockton to sign the papers.

After getting the money for the ranch, John went home to tell Mary about the sale. When she saw John and Tommy coming up the lane she wondered what was bringing them home. John was smiling, so she knew nothing dreadful had happened. One of the children always ran to open the gate, and John came galloping up to the steps of the house and sprang off his horse as he had not done for years. After kissing everyone he said to Mary: "Wait until you see what I've got for you!" He handed her a pouch filled with gold coins.

Before he could break the news to her gently Tommy spoke up: "Father sold the ranch."

"For only this much?" Mary asked.

"Of course not. I left most of it at Wells Fargo," John answered.

At first Mary was delighted—not because of the money

but because John would be home now. She had long prayed he would give up the river ranch. Now they would be a united family again.

John was very free with his money, giving each of the children a gold piece and telling Mary to buy herself some new clothes. Mary hid her gold. She would buy only what the eggs and butter and vegetables she took to market would pay for.

On Sunday they went to church as usual. A special collection was taken up for missionary work. John gave generously; after Mary saw his contribution she passed the plate on by without putting any more in it.

When the call was made for volunteers to preach the gospel abroad, seven men stood up. John was one of them.

Later on, after the fervor of the meeting passed, some of them reconsidered. Mary gave John scowling looks, hoping that he too would reverse his pledge. But however much she might dissent from his opinions, she would never chide him publicly.

On the way home she let him know her feelings. She said very little, but John knew she was furious. As soon as they got home and were by themselves he would hear from her.

He took more time than was necessary to unharness the horses and put them out to pasture, thus giving her time to cool off.

"How could you do such a thing to us?" she demanded as soon as he entered the house.

"What thing?" he asked.

"You know very well!" Mary said.

"If you are referring to the fact that I accepted a commission to go abroad, then the answer is very simple. Under the circumstances I could not do otherwise," John said. "I am sorry, Mary, that you do not have the same feeling that I have about this. It is a hope long deferred, and if it were not for your objection this could be one of the happiest days of my life. It is a dream come true," he said.

"If that is all you care about me and your children, then the sooner you go the better."

"Come now, Mary, you know why I feel obligated to go. I can no longer stand back and see our countrymen in England and Wales exploited by Brigham Young and his followers."

"Go on and go, I said!" Mary screamed at him. "Just forget about us. If we starve, that's all right, too."

"You give my very little opportunity to forget. I told you I left money at Wells Fargo. I'm sure none of you will starve. I will be back soon, and with the feeling of having done something worthwhile."

"Is there anything more worthwhile than supporting your family?" she asked.

"It is my family that is uppermost in my mind. It is the injustice that was inflicted upon them that impels me to try to save other families from the same fate."

"I don't think the Mormons are doing that now," Mary said, somewhat calmer.

"I am afraid you are wrong. Church policy is basically the same, only carried on in secret. Brigham is a smarter man than most people give him credit for being. He is determined to build an empire at any cost. He is a king among men, and if he has to use his people for pawns he will do it. I know because I was there, and now I have a chance to do something about it."

"John, you get so unreasonable when you get worked up over anything," Mary chided.

"Unreasonable! Do you call it unreasonable to want to spare others the treatment we had? Have you forgotten so quickly that we were held prisoners in Salt Lake City, that our friends were murdered, and that I was the next one on the list?"

"No—and I haven't forgotten that I have spent half of my married life in a wagon, either. Now that we have enough money to assure us a good future you want to pour it down a molehill," Mary said.

"Before I can plan on a future I must obtain a quittance from the past," John said. "Mary please, let's not quarrel. You know I love you, but my first duty is to the Lord, so I am going on this mission no matter what you say."

In reply, Mary went out and slammed the door.

John wanted to see Johnny before he left, so he made a trip to Stockton. He asked him to visit home as often as he could.

"I am putting my trust in you, Johnny," he told him.

While in Stockton he purchased himself some new clothes. He spent one gold piece after another until he had everything that made him look like a prosperous American. When he arrived home with his finery the children flocked around him and were impressed, but Mary looked on with an expression of disgust. It troubled John the way she was acting. Every time he tried to talk to her about it, they ended up quarreling.

The time passed quickly, and soon it was the day before John and the other men were to leave. A last big meeting was planned for them and their families at the church.

Mary had all of John's clothes ready. His shirts were starched and ironed and the stiff white collars were packed separately in a box with collar buttons and cuff links. Everything was folded and ready to go into his traveling bags. In repentance for being so ill-tempered with John she included a shawl she had crocheted for his mother. He was especially pleased over this generous act.

"I am sorry, Mary, if I have hurt you, but I couldn't rescind once I had made the offer to go."

"It will be hard to get along without you, and it seems to me the United States government has already done what you are going over there to do," Mary said resignedly. She had lost a lot of her anger over the weeks.

Since it was quite a little distance to the church, they covered their Sunday clothes with dusters and lap robes while they were in the carriage. When they arrived and were all dusted off, John took his new stovepipe hat out of the box and put it on, adjusting it very carefully so it would fit just right.

"Father looks like the President," Tommy said, and they all laughed.

One of the elders made a speech and had the missionaries sit up on the platform as honored guests. Their families sat in the front row.

"With great respect I give these men my blessing. I praise them for giving up their families and friends for such a long period of time. The journey will be difficult. I know they will carry out every detail of the mission entrusted to them. Let us send them on their way knowing they have our warmest and heartfelt wishes, for they walk in the light of the Lord. May God bless and protect them," he said.

Then he had each man stand up as he was introduced, although everyone at the meeting knew them all very well. John stole a swift glance at the front row where his family sat. It was a short meeting so the men could get on their way. Everyone shook hands and wished them good luck. John felt like a celebrity.

Mary had not realized when they left home that there

would not be another chance for her to speak to John alone. She loved him very deeply, and she had meant to convey that to him before he left. She was almost frantic as she pushed her way through the crowd to reach him. He took her hand, but he was kept busy acknowledging the good wishes and farewells of others. There was no way now they could have a conversation alone. Why hadn't she talked to him the night before in their bedroom? He had given her every chance.

The driver was there with the carriage, and they were told they must get on their way or they would miss the train. Mary had never ridden on a train, and that was another source of worry for her.

As John started to leave he turned, kissed her, and whispered in her ear, "Darling, it was your blessing and good wishes that I needed and wanted most."

Mary burst into tears as she kissed him good-bye. She could not speak. As she watched him leave she bit her lip to keep from running after him and yelling, "I love you, John!" But already his mission had taken him over.

CHAPTER THIRTY-FIVE

In 1873, accompanied by four other men, John David Griffiths sailed for Great Britain. They went as missionaries to preach the gospel of the Reorganized Church of Jesus Christ of Latter Day Saints. They planned to be gone a year or longer.

The journey from Stockton to the east coast was made by way of the Central and Union Pacific Railways. This means of travel certainly beat the covered wagons that John had previously crossed the continent in. The voyage across the ocean, too, was different. This ship was propelled by steam. John thought that without sails it looked as if it had something missing and wondered what would happen should the engine break down.

As they neared the shores of Great Britain John was very excited, and for the moment he forgot he was no longer a citizen. He began to tell the other missionaries, who had never been there, what a beautiful country it was.

"I have never seen another place quite like Southern Wales, and there are no finer people anywhere in the world than the Welsh," he said.

"John, I thought you were an American," a companion said.

"I am!" he hastily replied. He then remembered he had renounced forever all allegiance and fidelity to this country—but only in one sense, as there would ever linger devotion and pride for his homeland and his race. He often boasted of being a Welshman and of the fact that his children were of unmixed blood. It takes more than one generation to erase a man's heritage. But from then on he was more careful of what he said.

While they waited to disembark, John recalled a vow he had made the day he stood on the pier at Cardiff and first beheld the ship that was to take him to America. He had vowed that someday he would return to his country with money in his pocket and show the people what a person can do, living in a free country where no man is better than another.

"I am an American now and I will not have to step aside for any of them," he said aloud, grinning as he pictured a confrontation with the young lord who had made the scar upon his cheek.

"And I have money, too," he added, clicking the coins together in his pocket.

John was extremely anxious to get to South Wales where his family lived, but first he had a duty to perform for God, for his church, and for his own conscience. He would let nothing stand in the way of the mission for which he had come. He intended to enlighten the people as to the true state of affairs in Salt Lake City and to teach them the difference between that branch of Mormonism and the Reorganized Church.

John knew he looked his best, and that helped him to go about his work with the assurance he needed. He enjoyed having men of his own sort to talk to. They traveled through the villages telling the people at their doors or in their houses about the Book of Mormon and the pitfalls to watch out for should the Salt Lake missionaries approach them. They also held meetings and preached whenever and wherever possible. Often they would break up and meet later at a designated place to talk over what they had accomplished. It was their constant endeavor to lift the shame from the Latter Day Saints brought about by the church in Utah and to tell the people that Brigham Young was not the rightful successor of Joseph Smith. There was no one eligible until 1860 when his son, Joseph III, took the prophet's place.

They found it difficult to make the people understand that there were two churches bearing the same name. Even though "Reorganized" had been added to the group they represented they found that their church was still associated with the Salt Lake segment. The missionaries met with much vilification because of what the Brighamites had done and were still doing. On several occasions John encountered their missionaries preaching the Latter Day Saint gospel without hinting at the demoralizing practices raging in Salt Lake Territory.

John knew Brigham Young's dictatorship was as complete as the rein of nobility; the only difference was in arrogance. Brigham Young would humble himself to work beside the Saints to dig a ditch or drive a team or nail a board, but ultimate power was his and it was defended with force if need be.

Remembering his treatment in Salt Lake City, John approached his mission with zeal and vigor. He would walk many miles in a day and work far in to the night to inform people of the truth. He would relate to them the enormity of the crimes that he personally knew about.

"After I arrived In Salt Lake, the church that I was a member of made a rapid transition from bad to worse. Just the crimes that were inflicted upon me and my own family and friends would stamp Brigham Young and his followers with infamy even if there were no other charges against him," John would say.

John and many others had put so much of themselves into developing the city of Salt Lake that it was like having something they owned taken away from them. The temple had risen as if the men who toiled so diligently on it were hand in hand with God. They had worked under adverse conditions with pickax and saw and hammer. There was no equipment, only manpower. John could remember working day after day, prying on big boulders until he had exerted every ounce of his strength, feeling that if he pushed one bit harder his muscles would snap. The sweat would pour from his body, and then suddenly the boulder would slide into position as if at that moment God had placed his finger on it and moved it. He could understand why a man could worship a temple if he had helped to build it; it was something of himself.

The men were working their way toward South Wales when John received word from his sister that his father was failing fast and if he wished to see him alive he had better come soon. John left without delay.

As he neared Carew he tried to picture what his family would look like. It was hard to comprehend all the changes that had taken place in twenty years. His sisters, now grown and married, were girls when he saw them last. Two of his brothers had died, and his youngest brother was on the verge of death the last he had heard. The closer to his parents' home he got the more he longed to see them. He had tried to suppress such feelings before, because he had never expected to see them again. He could hardly believe it was a reality now.

When he approached the entrance the door was thrown open, and he was engulfed in hugs and kisses. His mother could not stop crying from joy. "I never expected to see you again, my dear boy!" she sobbed.

John was glad he had arrived in time to see his father and receive his forgiveness for disobeying him when he went to America.

"Oh, son, how I have prayed God to spare me so I could shake your hand and hear from your own lips that you bear me no grudge."

"Father, everything you warned me of came to pass. I did not realize how much I hurt you... until my own son, Johnny, turned against my plans for him and went his own way," John said.

A burden was lifted from both hearts. A few days after John arrived his father, David Griffiths, died in Christian faith and peace and was buried in the Carew churchyard, November 26, 1873.

John could scarcely believe the changes that had taken place. Everyone had aged beyond his imagination. It had been twenty-three years since that eventful night he had fled from his parents' home to sail for America in order to escape arrest for refusal to bow down and doff his cap when a member of the nobility rode past. There had been a sore spot in his heart ever since he had been forced to take a blow across his face and leave without retaliation.

The first place John went after his father's funeral was to look upon old Carew Castle. It had been built in approximately 1198. He stood looking at it as he had often done as a child, then walked around it without fear of being ordered away.

As he indulged in reminiscing, the thought came to him that this very castle had been his challenge during his youth. It had not been his hatred but his love for this old fortified watchtower that had caused him to rebel against being considered too lowly to be allowed to enter it or other surrounding castles of the nobility. He could look back now with the eyes of a man and see himself as he once was.

Previously the sight of this building made him feel mean and ashamed of his ancestry because he could not lay claim to the castle that his forefathers, the mighty warriors and kings, had built. Being ordered from the grounds around the castle when he had gone there to play had been the stigma of his young life. It had been his jealousy of noblemen, that had made him hate them and had caused him to fight against them later over their treatment of the lower classes in Great Britain.

He could see it all so clearly now. His pride and stubbornness against being cowed had prodded him on to self-education and to strive for perfection in all that he did. He often told his family it was no disgrace to be poor, but it was a disgrace to admit it.

His fondest dream had been to someday walk down the street,

impressing his relatives and old friends. It had not been solely for the purpose of preaching the gospel that he had come in his fine broadcloth suit and stovepipe hat.

Standing there now, gazing at the castle as an American, he found that his perspective had changed. He no longer felt humble or angry. As the realization of his folly came to him he laughed aloud. His whole being had changed. He felt equal to all, yet no better than any. It was only now that he fully realized what becoming an American citizen had meant to him.

"Oh, it is a great country, that America," he declared. "It can make a man feel so strong yet so meek."

John no longer felt animosity toward anyone or the desire to be boastful. He was glad he had visited the castle first and discovered the truth about himself. Now he would not belittle the things the people there cherished and honored as he had before. Let them have their beloved kings and queens; it made no difference to him now. It was the future of America he was interested in—something he and his children could build on.

John was anxious now to be going home, but his mother kept pressing him to stay. She was so old, and looked so frail since his father died that he remained a while longer because of her. But soon he became extremely lonely for Mary and the children. He was worried, too, because he had written Mary for money and she had not answered. He had not counted on missing them so much. He wanted to be home by spring.

As soon as the money arrived he went to Pembroke Dock where he visited his sisters Margaret Morgan and Phoebe Evans. Then he went on to Cardiff where he took the boat for home. He dreaded crossing the ocean even more than the long trip across the States to California.

This time John left his homeland with a warm feeling. He now had compassion for the man of noble birth. He had decided people were much the same the world over.

CHAPTER THIRTY-SIX

Charley and Rose were playing outside one afternoon when they saw a rider coming up the road. They told their mother, who knew it must be John. Everyone was excited and hurried into the house to get cleaned up before he got there. Mary had only enough time to quickly brush back her hair and put on a clean apron. May and Peggy and Tommy ran to meet him. The two little ones who barely remembered him remained on the porch with their mother.

Right away they noticed John's speech was slightly more British than when he left. It had been easy for him to recapture the accent and airs of his earlier life. He was wearing a handwoven black and white waistcoat his mother had made for him and had replaced the stovepipe with a British top hat. He looked quite dapper.

Mary felt humiliated because they were not better dressed for him. She had been in the garden all day and was trying to finish her work before cleaning up. At almost any other time she would have been tidy. But there was another reason why she did not rush into his arms as she really wanted to do. She waited for him to come to her first, because she was filled with resentment because he had stayed away so long—and because he had gone in the first place. John, with the girls' arms around him, hurried to where Mary was waiting, stone-faced. He had forgotten how displeased she was when he left and had expected she would be as happy as he was over his arrival. When he saw how indifferent she appeared he dropped his outstretched arms to his side.

"Where did you get this horse?" Tommy asked, appearing more interested in the horse than his father.

With such a greeting from Tom and none from Mary, John felt like turning around and riding away. His two youngest children did not even seem to recognize him. For the first time in his life he was at a loss for words.

"Well," Mary said, "you finally came home."

If she had meant to hurt him she certainly had. His whole being seemed to wilt. He was not sure now whether to take her in his arms or to get down on his knees. Finally he embraced her and kissed her passionately.

"I'll put the horse up for you, Father," Tommy said. This was his boyish way of showing affection. It sounded good to John to be called Father again.

"Oh, but it is good to be home. I have missed all of you so much," he said, and meant it.

He had not realized he had been gone so long until he picked up Rose. She had been a baby when he left; now she was walking and talking.

"I guess I stayed away longer than I thought," he said. "My youngest child doesn't remember me. But you, Mary, you haven't forgotten. Yet I haven't heard you say you are glad I am home," John said wistfully.

Just then the older children returned with John's luggage, asking permission to open the packages they knew were gifts for them. John picked up the smallest one and handed it to Mary. "I hope you will like it."

It was a beautiful crystal necklace.

"Here, let me put it on for you," John said.

"No, John. I don't want to put it on until after I have cleaned up," she said, and went into the house.

All the gifts he brought were expensive and carefully selected. All were as frivolous as the string of beads for Mary. There was not one thing they needed.

When in the bedroom by herself Mary began to cry. How could he be so blind to their needs? Only the week before they were so near out of food she had been forced to ask Sally for some dried beans to cook. The ones they had raised were all gone. They were so hungry that even before the beans were cooked the children started sampling them, and when Mary went to take them up for dinner there was little left in the pot but the soup. After experiencing such difficult times how could she be joyous over a string of beads?

Mr. Thomas and Sally saw that John was home. Later Mr. Thomas came over, carrying a bag of something. "Good to see you back," the older man said coolly, shaking hands with John. Then he turned toward the children and asked: "Where is your mother?"

"In the bedroom, changing her clothes," John quickly answered for them.

"Here, babe," Mr. Thomas said to May, "is something Grandma Sally sent for your supper."

Mr. Thomas then said to John, "You left your family in bad

circumstances. I hope now you can settle down and take care of them," and left abruptly.

John went into the bedroom where Mary was and slammed the door behind him.

"Now that your father has told me what a scoundrel I am perhaps you can explain what it is all about."

"I am sorry Father did that, but I had to ask him for help while you were away visiting."

"Why did you need help?"

"I had to have money to pay the rent!" Mary yelled.

"Rent? What do you mean by rent?" John asked.

"The man you sold to charged me rent."

"The agreement was we could live here until I was ready to move. He only wanted the land for pasture."

"The agreement was we could live here until you got a house built. Do you realize we have lived here over a year? I don't blame him for telling us to move or pay rent," Mary defended the man.

"You said John Henry quit school?" John said furiously.

"He had to quit and go to work to help us. I didn't want to borrow any more money from Pa," Mary said.

"How much do we owe your father? I have some money left. I hadn't expected you to send so much to me. I only wanted enough so I wouldn't be stranded if something happened on the way home," John said.

Mary explained between sobs how much her father had helped them—not so much in money but by giving them food and doing chores around the place that Mary could not do.

"Why didn't you write these things to me?" John asked her.

"You said not to write because you were coming home...and then you didn't come."

"I told you I might not be home until spring. I assumed you could get along that much longer. Now while I go over and set your father straight you get ready to go in to the store for whatever it is you need."

"It is too late to go today. It is time to eat supper."

"No, it is *not* too late. We will get there before the store closes, and it doesn't matter what time we get back. I don't intend to eat food brought in to us by the neighbors."

"Don't be hateful to my father...he meant well."

They were both very angry now. This was not the homecoming

John had expected. He was very ashamed of his family's situation. He was a proud man and never wanted his family to ask for or accept aid from anyone. He blamed Mary for putting him in this position. He believed she could have managed better, or at least she could have let him know.

John raised his head with the expression of one wishing to reestablish his authority. "I have come home with great appreciation from the church for the work I accomplished abroad, yet my own family treats me as if I have been off on some kind of lark. It was not pleasant walking in all kinds of weather day after day and holding meetings night after night. Sometimes I was without food as there would be no place to eat unless some kind person would invite me in. Yet I did not complain about my own discomforts while I was serving the Lord. The life of a missionary is not an easy one. Often all that sustained me and kept me plodding on was the thought of my family at home waiting for me. I expect the other missionaries' wives missed their husbands, too."

"The other men returned a long time ago while you stayed over there visiting around," Mary complained.

"For the main part I went to Wales representing the Reorganized Church of Jesus Christ of Latter Day Saints, and for what purpose you very well know. Yet in this first hour at home you have thrown it up to me several times that I went there for personal reasons. I spent very little time with my family in comparison to the time I put in for the church—but if it gives you pleasure to believe I went there solely to see my family I will admit I *was* extremely anxious to see them. While I was there I buried my father and bid my poor, sick mother good-bye. I will never see her again. Have I ever objected to you seeing your family?"

"No, John. No, you haven't."

"Then why is it such an awful thing that I wanted to see mine? I paid my own way. I was not indebted to the church."

"John, I am sorry. I didn't mean to be so cross. It is because we have gone without so many things we needed."

"Well, that is over now! Can't you look upon it as a sacrifice to the Lord? We will start out anew."

"You might be able to do that, but the reality of our want is still so great it will not allow itself to be forgotten," she answered.

"Mary, I want this bickering between us stopped. I cannot stand it. When you and I are at odds it is bad for the whole family."

John started to leave the room, sick at heart. Until now their life had been so full they'd been above arguing over little things like hurt feelings. There had been times when they did not know if they would be killed before morning, and they were always tender toward each other. In those days they never parted without an embrace and a kiss. There was always an understanding between them, and they were held by a bond so great John thought nothing could break it.

Before he reached the door Mary came running after him. "John, John, forgive me. I am not angry because you visited your family but because you stayed away so long. And I was hurt because you left me."

"I did not leave you, Mary; I was only gone for a spell. There was not a day I was not thinking of you. There was not a night you and the children were not in my prayers. I thought you would bear with me if I stayed a little longer with my folks and spent more money than I expected to," John said.

Mary came to him and put her arms around his neck. "I love you, John," she said and kissed him tenderly.

"Now, this is the kind of welcome I wanted."

All at once several voices were heard and it was plain that the whole family was coming into the house.

After talking to the children and catching up on what they had been doing, John walked across to see Mr. Thomas. He could not help noticing the improvements Mr. Thomas had made while he had been gone. His place looked well kept and prosperous. John could not help thinking he could have had the same if he had stayed there and raised sheep instead of gambling with the floods on the river ranch.

John was very polite to Mary's father but let him know he had in no way abandoned the responsibility of providing for his family. Mr. Thomas assured John that what he did for Mary was no more than he would have done for any of his other children. Both he and Sally were anxious to hear news from their families and friends, whom John had visited in Wales, and he stayed longer than he had intended, telling them of his trip. When he returned Mary had supper on the table and the children were already eating.

"I thought we were going to Lockford," John said.

"There is a cow to milk and chores to do. I just couldn't get ready and ride four miles to the store tonight," Mary replied. John stood silently, saying nothing.

"Supper is ready. The children were so hungry they couldn't wait for you any longer." Mary now sat down at her own place and waited for John.

He started to reject the supper, then thought better of it. It would only widen the gap between them. He sat down at his place at the head of the table, bowed his head, and gave a short prayer, proclaiming his love for God and thanking him for a safe journey.

CHAPTER THIRTY-SEVEN

Through Johnny, John soon found a way to bolster his family's sagging finances.

It seemed that someone Johnny knew owned a large ranch in Kernville, and because of an important engagement the man was not able to return and harvest the hay crop. He was going to let Johnny cut it and sell it on a percentage basis. Johnny asked his father to help him do it.

It sounded like a good deal to John, but he hesitated to leave Mary again so soon. He suggested that she go along. It was agreed that when Johnny got to Kernville and inspected the crop, if it still looked profitable, he would write back and they would come. His letter arrived saying the hay was waist high and ready to cut. So they set out for Kernville, taking the two youngest children.

When they got there they worked every daylight hour in the fields. All other chores were done after dark. John was thankful for the opportunity to make some money fast, and Mary was willing to help because she was anxious to get back to the other children.

Soon they were home again. The haying had been profitable, and John had money enough to look for a place to buy.

Land was easy to get with very little down. More people were interested in mining than farming, and many farms were idle. John found such a place at the end of Pacific Avenue in Stockton. This time he insisted that Mary look at it before he bought it; he wanted them both to be satisfied. Mary liked it because they would be near enough to schools that the children could attend without going away. Also it was not far from the cemetery where Fanny was buried.

John had decided while he was away that when he got back he would see that Mary had the house she had wanted for so long. She still had the house plans Johnny had drawn for her. They got them out and began to figure how much it would cost to build. Johnny promised to help the carpenter build it. He had not only learned building and architecture at school but also how to arrange finances. He explained about mortgages to his folks.

"Let us wait for the new house," Mary said. She did not want to go in debt, but John was convinced.

"We must have a house to live in, so we might as well build the one you want," he and Johnny argued. Finally she agreed. There was no doubt this time—she would have her house! The future looked promising.

Never did a house go up so fast. Everybody worked on it. The first night they moved in they could not bring themselves to go to bed. They had to walk around and admire it and put things in their places and drive one more nail in for this or that.

They were sure there was no finer house in town. It had five bedrooms upstairs, and a door opened from the hall out onto an upstairs veranda. There was one bedroom downstairs, a front hall where the stairway went up, a huge parlor, a dining room, a spacious kitchen, and a big storage pantry. Three sides of the house were covered by a broad veranda. Underneath a part of it was a cellar where milk and butter could be kept cool. The only problem was that the big house looked awfully bare with their scanty belongings, and there was no money left to buy furniture.

Mary was not as happy over the house as John had hoped she would be. She worried about the mortgage. "How can I feel that it is mine when it is not yet paid for?" she would ask.

"Don't worry so much. Plenty will come again, and peace will come with it," John would say to her.

He recalled that through all the hardships they had endured together Mary had been the one to keep up their spirits. Her uncomplaining patience had kept him steady. But ever since Fanny's death it had been hard for her to be cheerful. John found her crying, and he realized it was more than the debt on the house that was causing her grief. He talked to her about it.

"My dear, a little crying will put your heart at ease—but you must be more cheerful for the sake of the other children. We share the sorrow of losing Fanny, but it is our sorrow. We must not keep reminding the children of it."

He held her in his arms and after a while she said: "I know, John, you are right."

Happier days followed, and the future looked bright. John and Mary worked together again and were well pleased over the returns of their crops. When he saw her planting flowers he knew she was herself again. May was happily teaching her first school. John Henry had taken up politics and was off stumping the county with political speeches for the Republican candidate for the governorship of California. This was a disappointment to John because he had expected Johnny would get a job and help them pay off the mortgage. Then they heard he had run out of money and was working in Kernville.

Mary worried about his welfare, and nearly every day she would have May write to Johnny asking him about his health and well-being. Then at last a letter came.

The whole family enjoyed the letter. John laughed when he read it and said: "Johnny is twenty-one now. You will have to stop treating him like a child. I notice he signed his name J. Henry."

Tommy turned out to be the farmer and his father's help mate. As much as they encouraged him to attend school he refused to go beyond the fifth grade. He was a dreamer and liked to sit and think of far-off places, but he was content to travel only in his dreams. The little children were happy with a new pet, a brown and white Newfoundland big enough to ride up and down the road.

Mary began to spin yarn to knit into socks for Johnny. Men always need socks, she thought. She wanted to hurry and send them to him in place of a letter. It was plain to see he resented being written to so often. Besides Johnny chided her, in a gentle sort of way, about her misspelled words, but she knew that her knitting would be perfect. She had been sitting over her work for some hours when the door opened and Charley came in. He had been helping John irrigate.

"Father said in Oregon you don't have to irrigate."

A startled look crossed Mary's face. "What else did Father say?"

"Nothing."

Charley got down on the floor and began to wrestle with his dog, Cookie. After a while he said, "Father said it would be easy to go to Oregon."

Mary sat looking into space for a long time, then quickly gathered up her yarn and put the spinning wheel away. She went outside, and once in her garden, working, she threw off the strange feeling. It was nothing to get upset over. John was probably just making conversation with the children. Surely he wouldn't tear up roots and start traveling again. No one in his right mind would think of it.

But John was not just making idle conversation. For some time he had been nursing "Oregon fever." He had kept it to himself, as there was no use talking about it to his family. He knew Mary would never go while the children were small.

The gold rush was over in California, and lots of people were going north since better roads were being built and gold had been discovered in southern Oregon. It was said that the streams were full of the finest salmon and there were great forests of fir and pine and an unlimited supply of water. Such tales fired the imagination of a frontiersman who had the constant longing to see new lands.

Later that day Mary brought up the subject. "Charley was talking about Oregon today. I wonder how he knew about that awful place."

"I don't think Oregon is an awful place. In fact, from what they say, it is wonderful."

"Who says?"

"Oh, different ones I have talked to who have been there."

"Well, why didn't they stay there, then? It certainly doesn't interest us."

"I wouldn't say that. I hear they have opened up the Rogue River Valley to homesteaders. You can take up 320 acres of government land in Oregon. With Johnny now of age, together we could get 640 acres."

John went to great lengths to tell her all the advantages of moving to Oregon, but Mary knew it was John's love of adventure that really motivated him. Every time he met a frontiersman or saw a covered wagon he had a longing to start traveling. But this time Mary made up her mind to refuse to go.

The price of farm goods dropped, and it took most all they could earn to make payments on the mortgage. Tommy was growing up and beginning to talk of leaving home. Mary knew it was only a matter of time before he left unless they could start paying wages to him.

Mary wished John had never heard about a mortgage. She would not have had the nice house, but neither would she have had the worry. It was like having something and yet not having it.

Johnny could not find work near home, either, but the Southern Pacific Railroad was hiring every man it could get to work on the line going through the Siskiyous in southern

Oregon. One day Johnny rode away on his horse to Sacramento. When he returned he had a contract to get out several thousand ties for the railroad company.

He showed it to his mother and asked her if he should sign it. Mary would have nothing to do with it. Since the mortgage, she was afraid of any legal document. Johnny showed the contract to his father. It stated a certain price to be paid for the ties, how many, and that they were to be cut and delivered by a specific date. A map of the nothern country was spread out on the kitchen table, and John and the boys sat around it talking and figuring far into the night. Mary sat knitting. She heard but did not speak.

"I think it is better to go on our own than to be tied up by a contract," John told Henry.

The northern branch of the railroad was coming through the Rogue River valley. The two lines would meet somewhere near a place called Ashland. That tied in with what John had been wanting to do. If Johnny could get a contract for ties for the road going north there was no reason why they couldn't get one with the road coming south and get the land too. They could prove up on their homesteads and at the same time be getting out the ties. Everything seemed to be falling into place.

The planning went on for several weeks. The more they talked about it the more it seemed a reality. If it had been just a notion of John's, Mary would have known how to cope with it, but Johnny and Tommy and even Charley discussed it every waking hour.

May came home from her teaching job for the weekend. Johnny was the first to break the news to her about their Oregon plans. She sank heavily into a chair and burst into tears. Peggy and Rose, who loved adventure, were not at all upset. It was May and her mother against all the others.

"Hannah Mary, stop that crying!" John said, losing his patience. "What difference does it make to you whether you live in California or Oregon?"

She refused to answer, but eventually it leaked out that she had met a young man and was keeping steady company with him. Two against six was not enough, however, and the plans to go to Oregon kept growing.

John was afraid if Johnny and Tommy went they might not

select the best homesteads. But neither did he trust Tommy to follow later with the stock and the family. At last it was decided that John and Tommy would go first and find a place to settle.

Mary firmly believed that John was going through another spell of wanderlust, and if he got away from his duties for a while he would come back and be content to settle down again. She agreed for him to go but refused to sign any papers selling the property there, still hoping she might not have to move.

CHAPTER THIRTY-EIGHT

In the spring of 1882 John and Tommy, with a string of pack animals, headed north to Oregon. This time John was going farther into the wilderness. Their destination was over four hundred miles away. They traveled at a leisurely gait so they could view the country as they went.

The roads were dusty in dry weather and muddy when it rained. There was a great deal of travel with the regular run of stagecoaches and freight wagons in addition to the constant flow of settlers moving north and south.

It seemed as if the valley was endless, but after many days they could see the outline of the Cascades and several snowcapped mountains. Mount Shasta loomed 14,000 feet into the sky. They kept traveling toward it up narrow ravines where the river was lost in the chasms below. The forests appeared green and fresh, with pine and fir and incense cedar mingled with oaks and madrone.

Finally John noticed that the water in the streams was flowing the other way and knew they had crossed over the summit. They left the road to ride to a high rocky knoll where they could get a sweeping view of the country. They could see a broad valley far below them.

"Is that the Rogue Valley?" Tommy asked.

"No, we have another range of mountains to cross before we get to it."

They camped one night in the Siskiyous. Darkness fell upon them while they were eating their supper around a campfire. The heat of the valley had faded, and John soon fell asleep. Although Tommy had been assured there were no bad Indians along the route, the tales of their treachery were still fresh in everyone's mind. A breeze rustling the branches of the trees and an owl hooting in the distance kept him awake. It seemed as if they were so deep in the wilderness they had left all civilization behind.

The following day they came down out of the mountains where they viewed a narrow valley, already dotted with farms. They followed down the creek to Ashland Mills, then journeyed on to Jacksonville, the county seat and largest town in the valley. They set up camp nearby, but it soon became evident that they would have to move to a more remote location.

John found to his disappointment that most of the good farmland along the river had been claimed already, either by the O & C land grant or by other settlers. Much of the timbered land, up the branches of the Rogue, had been taken up for mining claims.

Settlers were pouring in from all over the country. On every stream they ran into other men looking, as they were, for land to homestead. Every other section belonged to the railroad company which was asking two dollars and fifty cents an acre. John decided to go farther down the valley. He took the old stagecoach road and followed it until they came to the river. This was their first sight of the Rogue.

"If someone fell into that maelstrom he'd have a hard swim to get out. It well deserves its name," John said.

He cautioned Tommy to watch his footing when he waded into it. They could see fish aplenty, and it was hard to get Tommy started on. They stayed that night near a little town on the opposite side of the river called Rock Point which consisted of a store, post office, way house, livery stable, blacksmith shop, and of course a saloon. There was also a schoolhouse.

On entering Haymond and Magruder's general merchandise store they found that it had a little of everything in it besides the post office. The people were very friendly, and John told them why he had come to Southern Oregon. The storekeeper told him there was land to the north, up Saradine Creek, that could be homesteaded. The Chinese had been in there mining but nearly all had gone since their diggings ran out.

The very next day John and Tommy headed up the creek. Although it was a small stream it ran year round. The storekeeper told John this, adding that many of the smaller streams which looked good now would dry up later in the summer.

The road followed the contour of the hills, and they kept climbing. There were many lizards darting in and out among the rocks. As they got higher they entered patches of timber, came out into natural meadows, then entered the timber again.

Finally John halted. He had passed several landmarks he had been told to watch for, and had almost begun to fear that he had gotten off on a wrong road when they came to the forks of the creek. Here they were to go east up the draw a short distance to where there was an open field on the hillside to the right. At this point they began to scrutinize the ground in search of the section corner.

Some of the ground was covered with good timber, and some was in natural fields or meadows, dotted here and there with clusters of huge oak trees, but most of it was rocky hillsides of chaparral, manzanita, and poison oak. It was not uncommon to see a rattlesnake sunning on a rock.

This was not the kind of place John had dreamed of bringing his family to. But there was plenty of grass through the woods for the stock to graze on, and the climate was so invigorating it seemed to give him energy. The water was cold and pure, and there was an abundance of it. In addition to the creek there were several good springs on the place.

Here fir grew besides pine, and fir was what was needed for railroad ties. Another thing in its favor was the possibility of gold. In every pan of black sand there would be a few cents worth of gold. He could hardly get Tommy away from the creek where he was panning for it.

After considering all angles, John staked his claim and sent the application in to the District Land Office. He also wrote for his family to come. He told them to take plenty of time on the road and to write and let him know about what day they would leave Stockton so he and Tommy could meet them and help get the stock safely through the Klamath district. The Indians seemed peaceable but some of them were not above stealing horses. He said to bring all the stock as there was lots of free grazing land. His next move was to start building a house.

After Mary received John's letter she knew the move was bound to come, so she started preparing for it. John might go farther on, but she was sure now that he would never come back. When school was out and May came home she was willing to move to Oregon. Jack Huber, the young man she had told them about, was going there, too.

But for Mary it was not that easy to leave. Her father and his family had followed her to Utah, then on to California, but he was too old now to start over. She knew she might never see him again.

He came in to Stockton when he heard she was going to Oregon, and it was a sad occasion as they said good-bye.

Mary delivered the papers for the sale of the place to the new owners. In order to get more work out of the children, Johnny made a game of getting ready, pretending they were an army and he was the general. They did everything he told them and quickly, without the usual back talk. Although the older ones were nearly grown, they had a lot of fun pretending. It reminded Mary of when she and her brother and sister prepared to come to America. Johnny had everything put in the wagon and ready to go so quickly that they were leaving sooner than she had written John they would come.

It looked as though the big canvas-topped wagon would never hold all the things they piled out to take. This time Mary was taking starts of her flowers and many other articles that John, had he been there, would have considered unnecessary. But to her children Mary's wishes were their command, and anything she put out to go was loaded regardless of its worth or weight.

When the load would get too heavy for one team, Johnny would hitch another. The last thing to go on was a crate of chickens. It would be quite a procession. They had it all planned. Riding ahead out of the dust would be Mary and Rose, driving a fine pair of trotters hitched to the surrey. Next would be the canvas-topped wagon with four horses pulling it. Charley was to start off driving, but he and Johnny would change from time to time during the day. There were four saddled horses and Johnny's own steed with a fancy Mexican bridle and saddle he bought while he was working in Kernville. Several horses and some colts would run loose along with the milk cows and forty head of young beef stock. The girls would ride the saddled horses when they were needed to help herd the stock, or when they tired of riding in the surrey.

With the last detail taken care of, they all lay down to get some sleep, but they were too excited. First one would waken, then another, to ask what time it was. Finally Mary said they might just as well get up and start.

After a quick breakfast they all took their assigned places. May and Peggy, mounted on their ponies, were to help Johnny get the stock started. They owned a couple of trained cow dogs that would do most of the work keeping the stock going and in line. Johnny seemed to be everywhere seeing that each detail was carried out as planned. At last the word was given to go ahead. Mary started, and Charley was no sooner heard cracking his whip and yelling for his horses to "Git-up" than he was yelling "Whoa" and pulling back on the lead team with all his might to keep from running into Mary and

Rose. It was still dark but light enough that they could see Rose running back.

When they had first started, her kitten had come to her through the damp grass, mewing piteously. She had picked it up and let it snuggle against her, talking to it softly as she climbed into the buggy, but when they started up the frightened kitten jumped from her arms.

The horses were impatient and the stock was getting out of hand.

"Come on, Rosie, let that cat go!" Johnny called angrily to her, but she refused to leave without her kitten. It took almost half an hour of calling and coaxing before it would come.

They took the main road to Sacramento, heading due north, and kept that direction for over two hundred miles before they hit the mountains. Almost every night through the valley there was a ranch where they could rent a corral and hay for so much per head for the stock. When he went through, John had made arrangements and sent instructions where to stop to Johnny. He told them definitely he wanted to meet them before they got to the Klamath River crossing. He did not want them traveling through that country alone. Mary kept at Johnny to slow down, to give John time to get there by the time they did, but Johnny laughed at her fears. It was the first time he was free to act entirely on his own, and he didn't intend to slacken their pace just so his father could get there to boss him.

After they forded the American River they started climbing the mountains. Mount Shasta looked different from every angle as they caught sight of it through the timber. It looked blue and cold in the morning, but it was shaded pink in the evening by the setting sun. It was the most beautiful scenery they had ever seen.

There were magnificent forests, and riding through them during the heat of the day they enjoyed the fragrance of sun-warmed pine and fir. They kept finding new kinds of wild flowers, and once they set up camp near a woodland meadow where there were wild strawberries. Not knowing what the next turn would bring added to the pleasure of the journey.

After they left the valley there were no more corrals to put the cattle in at night. They hobbled some of the horses (with the lead horse hobbled the others would not go far). The cattle were the hardest to keep from wandering away. Johnny had to be up a lot during the night, and he was getting tired. They had stopped playing games; there was too much work to do now. Johnny did not admit it, but he began to wish his father and Tom would come. He was afraid to trust Charley with the watch at night. He knew if anything went wrong, it would be he who would get the blame as Charley was not yet old enough for so much responsibility. He had to call on his mother to help him.

They crossed the Cascades and the great prairie which stretched out to the Klamath River. Still Johnny kept them going. Looking at the map John had sent them to follow, Mary could tell they were nearing the Klamath River. They had heard reports about the Indians, and she suggested again that they stop and wait for John. The children were so anxious to get to Oregon, however, that they talked her out of it. A few days later as they slowly moved along a rock ledge they could look down and see the Indians camped at the crossing, just as John had predicted. If Johnny was afraid he didn't show it.

Two of the beef cattle had become lame walking through the loose rock, so when Johnny got to the river he had Charley round them out of the herd near to the Indians' camp. He told a man sitting there they could have the lame stock if his people would help him get his outfit across the river. The Indians were glad to accommodate him. They took the surrey across on a crude sort of a ferry. The wagon, however, was too heavily loaded, so one of the men drove it across. This was done so easily that Johnny chided his mother. "See, you spend too much time stewing over things that never happen."

She did not offer praise, for she did not want him to become overconfident.

They kept going northward until, as indicated on the map, the route they were to follow turned west. They were all weary when they came to a farm where they could enclose the stock for the night and set up camp. Johnny talked to the rancher and found it was only thirty miles farther to Rock Point. The man also pointed out a better way for him to go with the stock so they would miss the town of Jacksonville. They angled across the valley on a road that reached the river at a point where they ferried across, saving both time and distance. Mary thought they should go the way John had directed in his letter, but Johnny was getting tired and cross. The West developed in a man the characteristics of authority and self-reliance, so Johnny, like his father, went the way he considered best. It was his problem to get them there, not his mother's, he thought.

"But Father might have started and he will miss us," Mary said.

"He wouldn't go far. You know Father. He would stop and ask everyone they met, and they would know in a little while that we had already gone through," Johnny told her. Mary didn't say any more.

After living all his life in the vast Sacramento Valley, Charley said that the Rogue River Valley looked hemmed in and that it wasn't as big as some of the ranches in California. They all agreed it was a pretty sight, however, with lush green foothills and wooded mountains all around it and Mount Pitt looming up as if it was standing guard.

They passed Table Rock where Indians' councils once had been held. They had a view of the entire valley and could see anyone coming for miles. After they got across the river and traveled down it a ways the valley narrowed and became so rocky they could not get down to the river. Not knowing they were so near they passed by the Saradine Creek road and went on to Rocky Point. It was only a short distance back, but it took a lot of manuevering to get the outfit turned. Most of the people living there came out to see what all the noise was about. The dogs did a lot of yapping at a time like that. The farther up Saradine Creek they traveled the harder it was for Mary to believe that John would settle in such a place; to her it seemed nothing more than a wilderness.

All at once Johnny, who was riding ahead, reined in his horse. Mary pulled up the rig she was driving. He pointed to a board tacked to a tree. On it was printed *J. D. GRIFFITHS*. They turned off the road and started down a steep incline to where they forded Saradine Creek. From that point they could see a building across and up the hill a ways. The door of the rude dwelling opened and there stood Tommy, transfixed with astonishment at the sight of them. They could hear him calling out with excitement:

"Pa, Pa, they're here! Pa, Ma and Henry and the kids have come!"

CHAPTER THIRTY-NINE

Mary looked at her new home and pictured a life of privation and loneliness. In the midst of the general confusion no one noticed that her eyes were filled with tears.

She walked away from the others and wandered toward the little creek. The sound of the water as it tumbled down the mountain over the rocks seemed to give her strength and reassurance. When John came to her she looked up, and the tears were gone.

"I wonder if we can ever make a farm out of this," she said doubtfully.

"We made a farm in the salt of Utah, and we had one in the path of two rivers in California, and one in the desert there, too, so I see no reason why we can't do it here in the green hills of Oregon. I know no way of judging the future but by the past. Come, let me show you the house."

But John did not need to point out the plan of the house; it was precisely what she had expected him to build. The same lean-to affair, hastily thrown together, that she had lived in for most of their married life. She could hardly tell where the house left off and the woodshed began. At the far end of the main room was a frame of double-tiered bunks filled with straw that ran clear across the room. These were the accommodations for the family. Tommy had already been sleeping on one of the top bunks; Rose and Charley quickly chose the remaining two.

May and Peggy reluctantly approached the other bunks. Both were remembering the home they had left in Stockton. They stood holding their nice clothes, not knowing what to do with them. There was no place clean enough to put them down and no place to hang them up.

They fell into each others arms and began to cry. John noticed and quickly said, "It's only temporary. I am working on a bedroom for you girls. Now that you have all come I will hurry and get the new log house finished." He was ashamed of the accommodations when he took note of what attractive young ladies they had grown to be.

Johnny looked in the house, then went out and put his bed roll under a tree. He slept there until he got a cabin built on the piece of land that he homesteaded up the creek.

It was plain to see that Mary was disappointed, but she was like that, John thought. While he enjoyed the new, it took time for her to become accustomed to it. He believed, though, that here in this sheltered valley with the placid stream winding below the house and the sunny weather she could not help learning to like it.

He could hear the two youngest children running, yelling, and laughing. At least they were happy, and Tommy had never shown such enthusiasm as he had here.

"Come, you all, and see the deer I killed. I got it hanging in a tree all skinned and ready to eat. Pa and I had some for dinner," John heard him say.

Tommy proudly displayed the gold he had panned from the creek. They were all interested in that. He kept them well supplied with fish and game. To him Oregon was truly the Land of Promise.

John was especially thankful that Johnny was satisfied, because when he was displeased he could be quite disagreeable.

May and Peggy had teacher's certificates and got the schools they applied for. Since they would soon be leaving, they did not express their dislike of the new home to their father. It was only Mary who had to adjust to this lonely, out-of-the-way place. She would agree with John that it was a beautiful country with its perpetual greenery, its flowers, and windless warm days, but the sight of bare cupboards erased the beauty of it from her mind. She could not eat the scenery.

John said it was like living in a park away from the hindrances of the outside world. He was quite happy. It gave him a sense of pride to stand in his yard and know he owned the land as far as he could see—all three hundred and twenty acres—as soon as they could prove up on it. He had a certain feeling of having gained what he had been seeking. Even if he failed here, he had the freedom to fail in his own way and not be dictated to by anyone else. It was not as it was in Wales where he was obliged to live according to someone else's plans, laid out hundreds of years before he was born.

John felt he had given his family more than riches—he had given them the heritage of America. But he did not expect his children who had never known anything but freedom to understand. Mary thought of John as being more or less a dreamer. Sometimes she would say he looked at life through a mist, ignoring realities. If there was no practical way to explain disappointment or sorrow or failure he would attribute it to the will of the Lord. Yet she could not honestly say he was a failure, because it was not riches that he sought. Adventure and faith and the joy of living a free life were more important to him.

Mary might have been more sympathetic to his view if there had not been a family to feed. One of them had to be practical, so hours before dawn each day she arose and got the children up and out to work.

Winter came early with a great deal of cold and wet. There was snow or sleet or rain almost every day for weeks, changing only to keen, driving winds or sharp frosts. Mary was glad that the log house with the big fireplace was ready to move into before the snow came and that there was plenty of wood. Old residents claimed the weather was unusual. The stock had not been used to it and, with the shortage of feed, many of the horses and a few of the cattle died of cold and starvation.

Later Mary said, "I hate to even think of the privations we all went through that first winter in Oregon."

The following year was not so bad. In the spring, Johnny secured a contract from the railroad company for timbers and ties, which made work for his father and the boys as well as himself. They hewed the timbers by hand and split the ties with a broadax, then hauled them to the railroad. With this source of income and May and Peggy both teaching school they managed to survive that first hard year on Saradine Creek.

Just when everything was looking brighter, Jack Hubert arrived from California and claimed May for his bride. It was another heartbreaking moment for Mary when her oldest daughter left for California. The first few weeks after she had gone were difficult; then letters came telling of her happiness and her lovely home, so Mary could not help being glad for her daughter's good fortune. Her wish now was that the other daughters would do as well.

Years passed. In all their lives together neither Mary nor John had ever had a major illness. They often worried about their children but never about themselves. So it came as a shock when John's health began to fail. A man who has never had an illness is less patient and accepting when it comes, and John was like that. He refused to take any precautions until he became so sick he was no longer able to get out of the house. He had developed a bad cough, and since two of his brothers in Wales had already died of consumption Mary was afraid he might have contracted the same dread disease. She persuaded him to go to southern California and spend the winter with May.

Preparations were made for him to travel on the newly built railroad, and Charley was to go along to help him get there safely. The trip seemed to weaken him more. May did everything she knew to do, but he gradually grew worse. She wrote her mother that the doctor said there was little hope for his recovery. Mary was getting ready to go to him when the word came of his death.

It was a cold winter day when Mary and Johnny and Tommy met the train and saw John's body being set on the depot platform. May and her husband had come on the same train and stayed until after the funeral.

John David Griffiths, age sixty-five, was buried at the Rock Point Cemetery. On his headstone Mary had these words inscribed: "To him the mists have cleared away."

But for Mary, reality still remained. There was no loud lamentation, but her face was set and pale.

After the first shock was over the family tried to bear up cheerfully. The children did all they could to make things easier for their mother. When Tommy picked up the pail to milk the cows, however, Mary rose and took it from him. "I want to do it alone," she said, and no one tried to stop her.

For all their married life she and John had gone to the barn to do the nightly chores together. As she walked along the path she could still see his footprints, and inside the barn she sensed his presence. She remembered so well how only a few days before he had become ill he had said to her, "Mary, as we grow older, perhaps the most important thing is to keep alive the love we have for each other."

It seemed odd, but now that John was gone she no longer coveted worldly riches. As she looked back she realized it was neither the rich nor the poor years that greatly affected her; it was the equal participation in the ups and downs and the faith they had in one another that had given them strength and courage and joy.

Mary lost no time in moving away from the homestead and the memories it had for her. Her children built a home for her in Gold Hill, a little settlement near the mouth of Saradine Creek. The house resembled the one they had had in Stockton, only on a smaller scale. They wanted her to be happy and live a life of leisure. They thought she would like that, but without conscious plan she slipped out of the house, found her shovel, and began spading up a flower bed. They were about to stop her when they remembered their father saying, "Whenever you see Mother planting flowers again you know that she is happy."

Mary did not put it into words, because it sounded so unfeeling, but her happiness came from knowing that once she had planted these flowers John would not be there to make her move again and leave them. Then she smiled and said to herself: "It is as it always was; he went first . . . and left me to follow."